THE CAREER OF
A RADICAL RIGHTIST

Kennikat Press

National University Publications

Series in American Studies

General Editor
James P. Shenton
Professor of History, Columbia University

SCOTT G. McNALL

CAREER OF A
RADICAL RIGHTIST

A Study in Failure

National University Publications
KENNIKAT PRESS • 1975
Port Washington, N.Y. • London

Manufactured in the United States of America

Published by
Kennikat Press Corp.
Port Washington, N.Y. / London

Library of Congress Cataloging in Publication Data

McNall, Scott G.
    Career of a radical rightist.

    (Kennikat Press national university publications.
Series in American studies)
    Includes bibliographical references and index.
    1. Radicalism—United States. 2. Right and left
(Political science) I. Title.
HN90.R3M28   322.4'2   75-14457
ISBN 0-8046-9099-5

TO MY PARENTS

CONTENTS

PART ONE   THE ORGANIZATIONAL STRUCTURE

1. **The Freedom Center in Perspective**   5
   Initial involvement   5
   Historical context   8

2. **The Sociological Nature of the Freedom Center**   16
   A characteristic meeting   16
   The leader and founder, Walter Huss   18
   The charismatic leader   22
   Maintaining continuity in rightist organizations   26

3. **Organizational Development**   33
   Organizational structure   33
   The history   39

4. **What is the Freedom Center?**   74
   Model for a social movement   75
   Sect or church   82
   Limits to growth   86
   Changing themes   88
   The sect movement   99
   Conclusion   106

5. **Financial Sources**   108
   The Eagle   109
   Advertising   110
   Job printing   111
   Films, tapes, and publications   112
   Freedom schools, Seminars and rallies   113
   Contributions and Contributors   115

PART TWO   THE PEOPLE

6. Birchers and Centerites: Accounting for Radical
        Rightism   121
    The John Birch Society   121
    The case of California   131
    The freedom Center   132
    An application   136

7. Who Are the Members and What Do They Believe?   139
    Age of members   139
    Community backgrounds   140
    Attitudes toward the social world   141
    Social class and social class backgrounds   145
    Family structure   146
    Religious affiliation and religious beliefs   147
    Political affiliation and voting   150
    Ideology   154

PART THREE   THE CAREER OF A RADICAL RIGHTIST

8. The Career of the Radical Rightist   167
    Predisposing conditions   169
    Facilitating conditions   172

9. The Future of the Right?   178

                    Appendix   183
                      Notes   187
                      Index   199

Part One
THE ORGANIZATIONAL STRUCTURE

1

THE FREEDOM CENTER
IN PERSPECTIVE

INITIAL INVOLVEMENT

Many questions have been asked about the Right in the United States. What kind of people belong to radical right organizations? Do they belong because they are frustrated status-conscious individuals? Do they tend to be fundamentalists? In trying to answer the diverse questions that have been raised, writers often turn to descriptions of the formal and observable structure of the organizations. Or sometimes they delve into the social and psychological backgrounds of the leaders and other easily identifiable members. This report presupposes that in order to understand how and why people have joined a given movement one should study them, not their leaders.

The data to be reported here are the result of a study conducted during 1964 and 1965 dealing with the sociological and psychological differences between members of such organizations as the John Birch Society, and supporters of men like Billy James Hargis and Reverend Carl McIntire. One of the subgroups in this larger sample of rightists was composed of a random sample of fifty-six active members of the Freedom Center in Portland, Oregon. (The total number of active members in this city and its immediate suburbs was approximately five hundred.) How this group came to our attention, and how we collected the data are of central concern.

THE ORGANIZATIONAL STRUCTURE

To say that a study is based on participant observation and to merely leave it at that, particularly when it is a study of a radical rightist group, is insufficient. One must know how the researcher managed his identity, and whether or not this management affected the study. Early in 1962, I heard about the group because the city's two largest papers and the local television stations had given a great deal of coverage to the group's request to solicit funds on a door-to-door basis for its anti-communist programs. At the same time, the group was sponsoring the film, *Operation Abolition,* wherever it could, and this often involved showing it at schools and colleges throughout the city. This film was an "interpretation" by the House Committee on Un-American Activities of the riots that had accompanied their hearings in San Francisco in 1960. At one of the showings the leader of the group appeared and, after hearihg him speak, I decided I would like to find out more about the organization.

I found the group housed in an old concrete building perched on the side of a small hill above wood-frame homes. The windows of the building were dark from the exhaust of the cars passing on the heavily traveled street on which it fronted. Across the street was a large cemetery bounded by a high cyclone wire fence. Down the block a fuel oil company parked its trucks. Around the corner there were small grocery stores competing for business with signs that proclaimed, "Open 365 Days a Year."

I met the leader of the Freedom Center, Walter Huss, and explained that I had come to pick up some literature, and find out more about the organization. It was soon apparent that it would be no simple task to become a participant observer in the movement. Huss was generally suspicious of college students because the group had been "infiltrated" by a student from the University of Oregon and exposed to the news media. So one needed to be cast in the role of potential recruit or believer. This meant being called on not only to repeat the dogma of the organization, but to show support for the group's cause by working in such ways as distributing leaflets door to door, selling campaign materials, stuffing envelopes, typing, and so forth. It also meant that any study of the organization would have to be prolonged. It would not be possible to simply join and begin hanging around the organization questioning members. My role, then, became one of a "seeker." I would simply try to be friendly to the members of the organization, read the literature they gave me, go to the meetings they asked me to attend, and help with minor tasks. Often it was possible to claim exemption from certain tasks because of school activities.

This casual involvement with the movement which I had initiated while an undergraduate and continued off and on while going to graduate school, lasted approximately three years. For instance, when I came to town, I would make a point of going to see Walter Huss and some of the members of the organization. Thus, when I came to the point where I wanted to actively involve myself in order to collect detailed information, I had three years of groundwork behind me. At this time I told Huss that I was working on my dissertation which would deal with the relationship between religious and political beliefs, and that I wanted to interview members of the Center for this purpose. His initial response was perhaps appropriate for he indicated that that seemed so obvious that it didn't need to be studied. I managed to convince him of the legitimacy of the study, however, and began to collect the data in a systematic fashion.

I noted earlier that a larger portion of this study presents material from a random sample of fifty-six members. This material was gathered by professional interviewers who were not associated in the minds of the members with the study I was conducting. This allowed me to have an independent check on the impressions I had of the members' attitudes. The study comprises, then, a survey research approach combined with participant observation.

One issue needs to be dealt with at this point. What are the implications of research where your real beliefs are not revealed to the subjects? A difficulty with participant observer research is that if it lasts over a long period of time, and your beliefs do not coincide with those of the people you are studying, it can generate hostility. If you want the good will of the people you are studying, you must adopt portions of their rhetoric and style. In my particular case, this meant I had to pretend to believe in political dogmas that I did not believe in, and participate in activities that I had not participated in before. But the strain of this sort of situation is mitigated to some extent by the fact that even if you don't feel any sympathy for the people you are studying at first, eventually you come to see them as fellow human beings and to like them. You may be opposed to all of their ideas, but you arrive at a better awareness of why they feel and act as they do. This is one of the main reasons for participant observation: it gives you a feeling of the internal dynamics of the group that cannot be acquired from administering questionnaires.

But all of the question has not been answered. What is a researcher's ethical responsibility to the people he studies in the fashion described above? I felt that participant observation would be the best way to study the organization. At no point in the research did I openly challenge a person's ideas, try to argue with him or criticize his life-style. In short, people's identities were not challenged.

Our concern here, then, is with an analysis of how and why people join radical right groups, and what the processes are.

HISTORICAL CONTEXT

At the time this study was conducted, the national primaries, and finally the presidential election, furnished the focus for most of the activities of the Freedom Center. The Freedom Center was responding, like many other rightist organizations in the country, to a changing world and a new role for the United States.

The early sixties saw the beginning of the civil rights movement, and the active involvement of white college students in protest. The United States had not won in Korea. We began to increase our troop strength in Vietnam, and college teach-ins against this involvement began. The Bay of Pigs was followed by Kennedy's blockade to force the Russians to remove their missiles from Cuba. Kennedy was assassinated. The world out there offered little in the way of order or stability. The reason why the United States had slipped from world supremacy and why there were civil rights marches was obvious to some people; it was because of a communist conspiracy. Confusing events needed simplistic explanations, and the Freedom Center offered through its programs and activities a means to handle a changing world. Like many groups on the right, the Center's dogma centers around what I choose to call the politics of despair. This is the generalized feeling that the social world is beyond one's control and that the best one can do is to cry out. Part of Wallace's political support stems from this feeling. Wallace may not be seen as a viable candidate, but he does seem to be a person who allows people to express their frustration and disappointment in the larger social order.

As we will see, the strength of the Center tended to be tied to events in the larger social world. It grew during the Goldwater-Miller campaign. Its support dropped off after Goldwater's defeat and picked up as people began to respond to the rise in student demonstrations during the late sixties. It fell off after there was a decline in the visibility of the protests. With Nixon's trip to China, the Freedom Center was able to gather support from the Right in opposition to Nixon's policies and their support for the conservative candidate, Ashbrook. With each election campaign, then, the Center has been able to renew its energies.

Rightist groups have always sought to reduce confusing contemporary events to simplistic explanations. This has been true throughout the history of conservative organizations whether we look at the Anti-Masons, the Know-Nothings, the

American Protective Association, the Ku Klux Klan, Coughlin and his supporters, Senator McCarthy, or the John Birch Society. The Freedom Center is no different in terms of its use of simplistic explanations. It differs in terms of its rhetoric which in this case tends to be a combination of fundamentalism and anti-communism.

As Lipset and Raab have pointed out, one of the things that rightist organizations implicitly, and sometimes explicitly, advocate when faced with conflicting opinions and ideologies is that the marketplace of ideas be closed down.[1] If politics is a situation in which different opinions can be heard and argued, then *anti-politics* is a system in which there can be only one truth. "America right or wrong!" is the cry for a closed society free of diverse opinion. Bunzel uses the term "anti-politics" to describe a politics that is essentially moralistic.[2] This means that a singular or monistic explanation for events is raised to the level of dogma. Politics becomes a matter of "truth" and not a question of integrating diverse opinions. This is why there is a close relationship between fundamentalism and radical right movements in the United States. Both fundamentalists and rightists see contemporary events in terms of black and white. Both believe there is one way to interpret events, and both see the world as essentially evil. "If every political issue is a doctrinal struggle between good and evil for man's soul, and there is only one revealed path to salvation, the market place must be closed down."[3]

How this monistic and moralistic bent in extremist groups is articulated is of basic concern. At rightist meetings, and in rightist publications, people are told that only "they" can save the country, that if "they" exercise their common sense they will do more good than idealists, liberals, and Communists. They are defined as being in possession of the ultimate wisdom. Radical rightists by virtue of being "the people" are in a morally superior position to the "government intellectual" who is removed from the people. Lipset and Raab refer to this as "doctrinal populism"—the belief that the people are right and that the reality defined by them is the only true one.

People who challenge radical rightist definitions of the world—they challenge them just by virtue of the fact that they have different opinions—are essentially *evil*. Why evil? Because the rightist believes first and foremost in a conspiracy theory. If people have different opinions and behave differently it is because they are part of the conspiracy.

This is the ultimate product of moralism rigorously applied, and the heart of the monistic impulse: error is arguable, evil intent is not; in the political process, error is admissible and legitimate, evil intent is inadmissible and illegitimate.[4]

A conspiracy theory allows a radical right group to see a variety of incidents from the same perspective. We lost in Korea because of the deliberate indecisiveness of politicians. We could have prevented missiles from being placed on Cuba by invading the island in force, but we were prevented from doing so by government officials who didn't want to win. The civil rights movements is communist controlled, and students demonstrate because of communist agitators. Whatever the event, there is a ready explanation for it.

The radical rightist deals with a changing world and status insecurity not by seeking new philosophies and solutions, but by turning to the past. The belief that morals, people, and life in general were better "then," is reflected in the desire to preserve or return to ways of life that are familiar. In some cases, this opposition to change stems from a desire to maintain a position of power and privilege, either real or imagined; real in the case of the wealthy person who opposed additional taxes for welfare reform, and imagined in the case of the lower middle-class white who believes that any gains made by minority members will be at his expense.

This feeling of status insecurity, or the belief that one can be displaced from his position at any time, is endemic to American society. This is why the Right has persisted, and will continue to persist, in a country that is subject to rapid changes through industrialization and urbanization.

Freedom Center members are somewhat unique, as will

be seen, in terms of the amount of status anxiety they feel. The Freedom Center is made up of people who are marginal in many respects. They are downwardly mobile, old, and come from the bottom of the class system. They are clearly different from a group such as the John Birch Society, which is essentially middle class. The Freedom Center members' class position is reflected in the dogma of the Center. It is more millenarian and pessimistic than that of the Birchers. Members almost uniformly believe that public officials cannot be trusted, that things are getting worse, and that there are political and religious truths that everyone must adhere to. As will become clear then, Center members will differ from other radical rightist groups not in terms of whether or not they believe in a communist conspiracy, or advocate antipolitics, but in terms of degree. Middle-class rightists are likely to be less despairing about the socio-political order.

As one reads about the activities of the Center members, it is necessary to keep the historical context in mind. It has always been the dispossessed, or those threatened with dispossession, who have made up the following of the Ku Klux Klan, the Coughlinites, and so forth. Who is being dispossessed will, of course, change as society changes. New problems give rise to new movements. The same populations will be tapped for membership, although it is not necessarily true that those who support a rightist movement at one stage in their lives will support a different one at another time. For example, followers of Senator Joe McCarthy did not automatically transfer their loyalties to conservative organizations that flourished in the early sixties. The point is that a rightist, or in this case a member of the Freedom Center, is not a unique animal. He does not differ that much from many of his fellow Americans who, under the proper circumstances, could be drawn into rightist groups.

As Ladd has indicated,

. . . it is at least doubtful that the activists of the Radical Right are more uninformed politically, more discontented, alienated or inclined to authoritarianism than are other large blocs of Americans who have never associated themselves with extremist movements.[5]

Stouffer was one of the first to demonstrate that, when it comes to a willingness to grant others broad civil liberties that are guaranteed by the Constitution, *most* Americans are seriously remiss.[6] If this is true, it is of the first importance to understand the mechanism by which an ordinary "Joe" is tipped over into political activism, on the right. Our task, then, in this work is to explain how and why a person joins a particular group.

The Freedom Center, again like most rightist groups, will be seen to be in opposition to current office holders. This opposition to whoever is in power stems from belief in a conspiracy. It is, of course, easier to attract a number of adherents to the organization when those in power can be identified as "leftists." Being a Democrat is usually a sufficient criterion. When a person such as former President Nixon is in office the situation changes. The Center can generate some support for an Ashbrook, or, more likely, take advantage of the support already there, and bring people into the Center to take part in activities designed to oppose administration policies. But the support for the Center is not nearly as large as it was when President Johnson, identified as a liberal (especially in terms of his domestic policies) was running against Goldwater, who was clearly identified as a conservative.

The theme of anti-communism, coupled with a conspiracy theory, offers a means by which members can be attracted to a group. Anti-commuunism is, for some, part and parcel of the religion of America. To oppose the American Way of Life is sacrilegious. Anything which challenges this Way is suspect. This generalizing allows rightist groups to be opposed to ideologies and ways of life, then, rather than to specific groups. This is important, for most movements have a more identifiable, although less fluid and ubiquitous enemy. Whatever threatens the rightist, whether it is minority movements, college students with long hair, inflation, or welfare legisla-

13

tion, is a threat to the American Way of Life and is opposed by the dogma of the movement.

Smelser, in analyzing the development of social movements, argues that unless there is an identifiable cause for a specific problem there will be no movement, but hysteria. Hysteria is the belief that there is some ambiguous destructive element in the social order.[7] The result is a witch hunt, a search for those with impure ideologies. Many of the activities of the Center and other extremist groups center around an analysis of the ideological positions of various politicians on issues from sex education to demilitarization.

Nevertheless, a vague conspiracy theory is usually not enough to engage people's attention. A certain amount of backlash has been necessary.

. . . In American history, the backlash targets have often fitted neatly into the nature of the conspiracy theories. Anti-Catholicism and anti-Semitism, in particular, have been able to provide both an identifiable group of people and a suggestion of arcane recesses. But right-wing extremist movements have always had to invoke some backlash targetry, whether or not it fits the ideologues' conspiracy theory, in order to engage a broad national audience.[8]

Rightist movements at different periods can be distinguished by examining *who* the target for their enmity is. At one time it was Catholics; at another time it was simply immigrants in general; and for many Center members it was minority group members.

We see, then, that rightist groups offer a variety of specific means to achieve a vague end. The John Birch Society, for example, has at different times urged its members to seek the impeachment of Earl Warren, to "get the U.S. out of the U.N. and the U.N. out of the U.S.," to support their local police, and to support all efforts to end lawlessness and immorality. The Freedom Center, too, offers its adherents a variety of activities and social issues. The members of various rightist groups seldom accept or adhere to the range of attitudes and opinions offered by the group. Members selectively support specific dimensions to bolster their own social needs. One person may pick up on latent anti-Semitic and overt anti-black attitudes expressed in an organization, while ignoring such issues as opposition to fluoridation. What is involved here is expressive politics, to use Gusfield's terms.

. . . political action for the sake of expression rather than for the sake of influencing or controlling the distribution of valued objects. The goal of the action . . . is not a "solution" to the problems which have generated the action. Politics, in this usage, is a means to express how the actors feel about the situation.[9]

Thus, when one looks at the political activities of the Right he must be attuned to the fact that the symbolic meaning of the action is more important than specific economic and political goals. Action becomes a way of dealing with alienation and anomie. The central purpose of political action for a Centerite is the affirmation of primary ties.

The contemporary radical rightist is a person who has more of a stake in the past than he does in the future. He is a person who does not have a strong ideological commitment to democracy. He would rather see the marketplace of ideas closed down and the dominance of a "correct" political and social philosophy. The historical pressures that have contributed to the growth and development of rightist organizations in the United States have not necessarily abated. In fact, continuing urbanization, economic insecurity for the aged, and an increasing number of lower middle-class whites support a situation in which status and the future are insecure. How insecure Center members are will be seen in the following chapters.

2

THE SOCIOLOGICAL NATURE OF THE FREEDOM CENTER

A CHARACTERISTIC MEETING

General meetings are usually held on a Sunday afternoon beginning at two o'clock. Members arrive in older American cars or get off the city bus across the street. No one comes in a taxi. The people come in twos and threes and enter the building.

Downstairs they see people they know, give a wave of acknowledgment to some, stop and talk to others. Some look around at unfamiliar faces, others help move equipment around so that the meeting can begin.

The Pledge of Allegiance, the national anthem, and a prayer—bringing forth "Amens" from the audience—begin the meeting. There seem to be more women than men present, and some married couples. Most of the people in the room seem to be in their late fifties and sixties. Inexpensive flowered hats are worn by some of the women; most wear housedresses. Some of the men wear suits, but with open-collared shirts.

The speaker has been introduced and a short ripple of applause greets him as he approaches the podium.

Although the actual events occured some time ago, this chapter and what follows are written in the present tense for the sake of clarity.

"I'm so happy that I can be here to talk to you folks today, about communism. . . .

"The Communists want to destroy us . . . you and me . . . they want to take away our freedom. . . .

"Amen. . . . That's right!" say voices from the audience.

"The Communists are all around us. . . . They are doing everything they can to win the battle. . . . We must turn to God and His son, Jesus Christ, if we are going to win. . . . We must turn the nation back to God."

Certain themes emerge as the speech continues.

"Our government is turning down the road to socialism. . . . The word of God has been taken out of our school rooms. . . . Thet idealists and liberals are leading this country down the road to communism.

"Our national debt is higher than ever because of these government spending programs. Our taxes are being increased. Decent men can't make a living in these times. . . .

"Our school system is rotten to the core. They are teaching Deweyism, Freudianism, and sex education in our schools. Our teachers are not teaching our children about their precious heritage. Our children are being led astray."

"Yes, Jesus; you're so right. Amen."

After the speaker has finished and the applause has stopped, Walter Huss, the director of the Center, addresses the audience.

"The battle for freedom is never ended. Our precious liberties are being whittled away a little each day. We must act now. Every one of us must make sacrifices. We must each do as much as we can. We need to expand our operations here at the Center to fight the deadly menace of communism. Won't you please help us? Won't you please give what you can?"

A prayer is said, paper cartons are passed down the aisles, and the meeting is over. Some people stay and talk.

THE LEADER AND FOUNDER, WALTER HUSS

What kind of person runs the Freedom Center? Walter Huss is a reserved, quietly smiling man. When not appearing in public he can be found in suntans and a faded cotton-plaid shirt; in public he wears neat inexpensive dark suits. His hair is closely cut and he is never unshaven. At first glance, he could be any unassuming businessman. In the Center he can be found bustling about with papers in his hands, making phone calls, setting up stories for *The National Eagle,* the organization's newspaper, greeting those who have come to the Center, and directing the activities of the volunteer help.

But Huss is a harried and suspicious man. He is careful with those who ask questions, and hostile questions are met with hostility. Any person could be a Communist, or perhaps a dupe of the Communists. If a student questions Walter Huss and challenges his position, the student is accused of being naïve and uninformed.

Huss is energetic, alert, resentful of criticism, and overwhelmingly *dedicated.* He works long hours and drives himself from one day to the next, because there is always something to be done. Even when he was ill in April 1965, he was still active. From his sickbed he took notes, wrote out plans, and talked about the things he would do as soon as he was able. His dedication and his dogmatism work together. One plan is right for him. One approach is correct. He is a militant Christian anti-Communist. He is unyielding, he is authoritarian, there is nothing in our society that is none of his business. He wanted a full investigation of the sex scandals at the University of Oregon. He reprinted and circulated thousands of copies of selections from a "dirty poem" published in a campus magazine. When he heard that certain University of Oregon faculty members had held a reading of Allen Ginsberg's poem, *Howl,* he wanted to know where he could get a copy because, he explained, there had been many requests for the poem and he wanted to reprint it and send out copies so that people could see what was going on at the University. His concerns, however, are ultimately much broader than this.

Walter Laurence Huss, president of the Freedom Center, Inc., was born in Portland, Oregon, on May 19, 1918. He attended a local grade school and graduated from Benson Polytechnic School. To help pay his expenses at Benson he worked as a janitor's helper in the public school system. In 1941 he married Rosalie Johnson of Albany, Oregon, of whom a Center member later stated, "Rosalie Huss is a real sweetie. The whole organization depends on her. If she wasn't around the whole thing would collapse." Prior to his induction into the service he was working as a hull draftsman on navy ship construction. At this time he took courses in engineering and drafting, and was finally advanced to a senior classification. After his induction into the army in 1944, he served as head of the drafting section in the corps of engineers of the Third Combat Battalion and witnessed the allied invasion of the Philippines and the occupation of Japan. He was discharged in 1946.

Several of his overseas experiences made deep impressions on Huss so that he felt "called to the ministry." These experiences included helping to reestablish the bombed-out Evangelical Church of Davao in the Philippine Islands, and personally helping the various Chinese, Japanese, and Philippine people he encountered. He enrolled in the Life Bible College of Los Angeles, California, in February 1946.

Although not a licensed engineer, in Los Angeles he worked his way through the Bible college by serving as a mechanical engineering designer and draftsman for Lopker Engineering and Ralph Phillips Engineers of Los Angeles, and in his senior year at Life Bible College he served as an associate pastor of the Goodyear Foursquare Church in Los Angeles. He entered the ministry of the International Church of the Foursquare Gospel, founded by Aimee Semple McPherson. He mentions that in preparing for the minnistry he studied "the Hebrew and Greek languages, history, and developed talents in music and other fields, like public speaking."[1] He graduated in June 1950, and accepted his first appointment to the pastorate of the Cave Junction Foursquare Church in July 1950. (Cave Junction is a small community in southwest Oregon.) That same fall, the church burned to the ground and services were conducted on a temporary basis.

Seeking a new pastorate, Huss was transferred to Eugene, Oregon, home of the University of Oregon, to pioneer a new church for the Foursquare Gospel Organization. During this time he also operated his own sprinkling design and installation business, and worked as a draftsman for a local utilities company from October 1952 to May 1953. He left their employ in May on a leave of absence, but did not return. His personnel record indicates that he was "a good draftsman, but [his] personality did not fit in."[2] When questioned, some members of the personnel office recalled that he was not well liked by other employees. A secretary said he was disliked because "he tried to convert everyone. . . ."

During the five years he was pastor, Huss attended the University of Oregon where he took a number of education courses. He ranked in the top fifth of his class, but his classroom behavior was not that of the ordinary undergraduate. One of his teachers reports that Mr. Huss would frequently argue with him, and "quote scripture to support his arguments."[3] During this period Huss was instrumental in founding the Emerald Empire Christian School in Eugene. An ex-member of the school's board reports that Huss was one of several men who helped start it, and was also superintendent for a year. He also served as the secretary of the town's Ministerial Association, appeared on pastoral radio broadcasts, and served on the board of the Eugene Youth for Christ.

Huss then became involved in the larger area of Christian education as the western representative for the National Association of Christian Schools. He traveled extensively throughout the West, promoting the idea of private Christian schools. In 1956, wanting to do something "to further promote Christian education," he helped form a corporation called Oregon Christian Schools, Inc. As Huss noted of Salem, the town in which they located, they were "blessed with a Christian high school, but not a grade school, so we undertook to open a grade school."[4] Later, this organization was to become the springboard for the founding of the Freedom Center.

Huss was involved in other activities. The files of the State Board of Health indicate that he was licensed as a journeyman plumber from 1956 to June 30, 1960, and was operating the A.B.C. Plumbing and Irrigation Company. Two officials from the Commission of Public Affairs in Portland made a trip to Estacada in 1961 and interviewed several persons. Most of the people seemed to agree on several points. Huss had made himself unpopular by overcharging on plumbing jobs. An attorney for Estacada also added that in his opinion "Huss was very glib for a plumber, very religious and he liked to adopt a persecuted attitude." He noted that Huss had purchased the plumbing business from a local resident who eventually had to take it back.[5] Huss was licensed as a sewage cesspool worker in 1956 and 1957, and drove a school bus. During 1959 and 1960 Huss was serving the Evangelical and Reformed Church in Salem, Oregon, as their supply pastor and was also chaplain for the Civil Aeronautics Board during this time.

In 1958 he attended a special school for anti-Communists in Long Beach, California. It was during this week-long course in December 1958, that Walter Huss was "shaken from any tinges of complacency" about the possibility of a communist takeover, "and returned home to Salem, Oregon, believing that this wealth of information should have widest circulation."[6] This ultimately led to the founding of the Center.

Huss's occupational career has been outlined in some detail for several reasons. First, Huss had presented himself as a self-made man. He had learned several trades, and had not stopped learning. When he began to run the Freedom Center full-time, it was necessary for him to learn the numerous and complicated processes of putting together a paper, *The National Eagle.* He also had to master the use of sound equipment for his radio program and public meetings. Huss is a dynamic person with what would seem to be a high level of practical

21

ingenuity. The other thing to be noted about Huss is, of course, the sporadic nature of his career. This pattern of activity will be seen to have influenced the development and decline of the Center.

THE CHARISMATIC LEADER

Walter Huss has been called a crackpot and troublemaker. The people of Portland, if they knew of Huss and his work, tended to disapprove of it. And it was not only the people whom Huss might term leftists who did not approve of the Freedom Center. In several cases, people who were members of the John Birch Society and other patriotic organizations questioned the methods employed by Huss to fight communism.

A specific issue, to be dealt with at length later, brought the Freedom Center to the attention of many people. Briefly, Huss appeared for the Center before the city council to request permission to solicit funds for their work in the city. The final part of these hearings was televised, and there was a certain amount of public reaction. The following quotations are from letters written to members of the city council after the latter denied the Center the right to solicit funds in the city.

A student wrote saying, "May I congratulate you on your objectivity and humanity in refusing to grant solicitation rights to the Freedom Organization in Portland."

Another person questioned the ideology of the group by stating, "Anti-communism is a fine motive, pro-democracy is more admirable, but crackpotism (including neo-McCarthyism) is poisonous to the misguided fools who look to it for salvation."

Letters in support of the city council's decision came from an ex-president of a state university, an architect, several attorneys, college professors, an advertising agency, several ministers, a United States congressman, students, labor officials, housewives, and many other citizens of the city and the surrounding metropolitan area.

Huss has been attacked at one time or another by most of the major papers in the state. Regarding one editorial,* written by Eric Allen, editor of the *Medford Mail Tribune,* Huss wrote demanding a retraction—which was not given—stating that:

You have sought to convince your readers that I am:
The Portland scandal monger
Ultra-right winger
Character assassin
Would-be politician
That I make charges (which are outright phonys) [sic]
That I associate with dirty-minded colleagues.[7]

What kind of a leader is Huss? How is he perceived by members of his organization? Has he sufficient charisma to maintain the strength and continuity of the organization? There is little doubt that Huss was discredited by a significant portion of the population in the Portland metropolitan area. But, discreditation by the general community does not preclude charisma. Charismatic leaders have been labeled as malcontents, rebels, and worse. It is the *followers'* attitudes that must be taken into account in determining whether or not a particular individual has charisma.

In the case of Huss, the element of persecution, whether real or imagined, played a significant role in how he was seen by his followers. Some of the qualities which Max Weber saw as characterizing the charismatic leader were: (1) devotion to him by his followers because of his extraordinary qualification; (2) the belief that he is a genius and transcends the mundane world; and (3) his qualities as a revolutionary force.[8] The element of persecution allows the leader of a movement considerable freedom to develop a set of circumstances that will allow him to define himself to his followers, and be seen by them, as a charismatic leader.

Any group with an identity—which implies some cohesion and interaction—has an ideology which expresses the

---

* (The editorial concerned Huss's activities which had to do with what we will call the *Northwest Review* issue, to be referred to in some detail later.)

uniqueness of the group's position and the validity of its ideology. The ideology can be anything. It may be as general as a caste ideology explaining why the members of a particular caste are at the bottom of the social system,[9] or it can be as particular as the ideology of a delinquent gang which allows them to define acts of hostility against a local merchant as "evening the score." And it does not matter if the dominant community sees things differently than the group in question. In fact, as Festinger et al. have shown in their discussion of cognitive dissonance, if a group is strongly committed to a particular position and that position is attacked, instead of changing its position, it adheres even more strongly to it.[10] The members of the Freedom Center saw themselves in constant battle with leftists, Socialists, idealists, Communists, and freethinkers. The cry of "persecution" became a rallying point for the movement and a source of support for their image. The very act of seeing oneself as persecuted, then, helps to more clearly define the boundaries of the group and isolate oneself from the larger society.

As we have noted, the element of persecution allows a leader of a movement considerable freedom in the way he presents himself. He can claim that he is a revolutionary force if the dominant community reacts against his ideas. Robert Welch, Billy James Hargis, Richard Cotton, Carl McIntire, and Walter Huss all use this technique. They state that because numerous leftist groups and individuals attack them this proves they are "getting at the Communists." For example, Huss cited Herbert Philbrick:

Herb Philbrick, the famous counter spy [sic] for the FBI who posed as a Communist for 9 years, told me just last Wednesday, "Walter, the fact that you are getting this kind of treatment and resistance is crowning evidence that you are hurting the Communists. Keep up the struggle."[11]

The belief that a leader is a genius and transcends the ordinary world can also follow from the claim that he is persecuted. It is said that he is attacked merely because he is different, and that he is different, not because he is inferior to his fellow men, but because he is superior. In enumerating his activities when he appeared before the Portland City Council in 1961, Huss felt called upon to explain his activities.

Why was I out doing this? I think the best appraisal of my activities is in some of the letters which I have not solicited, but have come spontaneously, from heads of service clubs, heads of schools, from churches, ministerial associations, that sponsored area-wide activities in which I was the principal speaker, and the like. But this year, of course, is going way beyond last year, and this with all *the smear campaign we have had to face, and I face it in Christian love,* because I realize that, *like Christ* as he *looked down at the people around him, they didn't realize what they were doing;* and also, when Stephen was martyred, he prayed, because these people didn't realize what they were doing in *silencing a voice which was for their benefit and aid and comfort.*[12]

The final element that Weber saw as contributing to charisma was the devotion of the followers who believed their leader to have extraordinary qualifications. It is here that we can most clearly see how Huss diverges from the traditional charismatic leader. He was recognized by his followers as a dedicated, hard-working, and self-sacrificing man, but had difficulty in eliciting total commitment.

In a questionnaire Center members were asked to name someone living or recently deceased whom they would consider a "great American." In only two instances did respondents name Huss, as we might expect them to do if he were regarded as a charismatic leader.

Another indication that Huss was not considered a charismatic leader was the amount of support he got from his followers during his unsuccessful campaign in a primary election. He ran as the Republican candidate for Congress in November 1963. One manifestation of the followers' support was their contribution to the political campaign. The number of Center members in the Portland metropolitan area was over a thousand, as measured by those who actively supported the Center in terms of volunteer labor and contributions. (This does not include all of those who were on the mailing list for the area.) Out of this total population, Huss received $1,521 in contributions for his campaign. Of the twenty-five contributors, twenty-one lived in the Portland metropolitan area. Most of the contributions were small, around $10 to $20, although two people gave $100, and a local woman contributed $535. This does not represent a strong base of appeal.

Regarding this election, a member of the Freedom Center said that he had not contributed to the campaign because he did not believe that Huss had a very "realistic approach to political problems." He went on to say that "Walter said he had prayed and God had told him what to do, but I don't believe it." Another member when asked about Huss's campaign said, "It's pretty hard to agree with him a lot of the time. He is much too rigid in his beliefs."

If a person is viewed as a charismatic leader by his followers, another indication of this would be his ability to control them and direct their activity. Although we will elaborate on problems of control in the following section, suffice it to say that Huss was often faced with problems such as people going their own way, dropping out of the movement, deciding that they would not participate in a particular program, and so forth. Huss was viewed as human and fallible by his followers. The dimension of persecution allowed him some freedom in shaping his image for his followers and defining the group's boundaries. It was not a sufficient criterion, though, to allow him to command the total loyalty of members.

MAINTAINING CONTINUITY IN RIGHTIST ORGANIZATIONS

We have already noted that there was a problem of controlling members of the Freedom Center. When this study was conducted, practically all of the labor done for the Center was by volunteers over whom there was little or no control. If people were tired, they went home. If they wanted to go shopping, instead of fighting communism by working at the Center, they went shopping. After the Goldwater-Miller campaign the number of Center members who were helping at the Center dropped off. This was in spite of Huss's pleas that the work was not over, and that there were other issues to be dealt with. Meetings were called, but only a few attended. There were no sanctions that could be imposed. A rightist does not feel threatened by being denied access to a particular group. He can just as easily shift his loyalties to another rightist group, or any other available opportunities that present themselves. For instance, after the Goldwater-Miller campaign many women increased the amount of time they spent with religious organizations of which they were already members.

The point is that the movement must appeal to the members, not the members to the movement. The sheer number of organizations which are clamoring for the time and money of the same people is a factor which weakens the entire movement. Austin T. Flett, head of Help Fight Communism, Inc., remarked to me that this was the whole trouble with the Right. "Everybody is in it for himself. . . . Some of the organizations are just business concerns, and nobody is going to give up his business." This was illustrated in a discussion with one Centerite. When I questioned him regarding how much money he contributed to the Center, he said "none at the present." He clarified this by noting, "I used to give quite a bit of money to Walter, but now I contribute a little to Hargis, Smoot's program, and the 20th Century Reformation Hour. You understand, there is just so much money to go around." This is also one of Walter Huss's more frequent complaints. As he has said, "People just don't realize that they have to support what is going on here in the state, instead of always sending their money some place else."

The Right in this country is not unaware of the problems that are involved in trying to coordinate the efforts of their members. The Reverend Billy James Hargis called a meeting of leaders of rightist organizations on March 20, 1962, and invited representatives from approximately seventy-five rightist organizations to meet with him and coordinate their activities. But his invitation carefully spelled out "coordination," not "unity."[13]

Hargis was quite aware of the desires of various rightist leaders. Each leader, organizer, or owner of a printing press behaves as if he has the "message," as if he alone were going to lead the country out of the "mess the leftists and liberals have got it in." Robert Welch of the John Birch Society tells his followers that the society is the most "cohesive and effective" of all the rightist organizations. He praises the members for being part of an "effective political organization that gets things done." Carl McIntire tells his followers how *they* are winning the fight against the leftists. Schwarz tells those who attend his Christian Anti-Communist Crusades that *they* can win the battle if they will listen to the lessons. Charles W. Burpo said in the introduction to his book, *An Angry American,* that *he* is awakening the continent to its problems. Each author, editor, and leader has his own program. He is committed to it for both ideological and economic reasons.

A main problem that the Right has in coordinating its efforts has to do with who is and who is not a member. Is the person who contributes to Hunt's program, "Life Line," a member? If you listen to all of Hargis's broadcasts, but never subscribe to any of his publications, are you a member of his organization? If your name is on the mailing list for the 20th Century Reformation Hour, does this mean you are a member? In attempting to answer these questions, one is faced essentially with the same program that arises when one tries to decide how many members a church has. There are those who attend irregularly; there are those who were baptized into the church and have ceased to attend frequently but are baptized members of another congregation.[14] The churches realize that there is a "free-floating" body of people who are potential members. They must attract these members in some way. This is a situation peculiar to the United States, where the church is ultimately dependent on the members for sources of revenue.[15] Consequently, the members have a form of control over the churches. They can withhold their attendance and in so doing withhold the funds that are necessary to operate the church or parish. The minister is dependent on his flock; he must appeal to them, not the other way around. It is true that a person can be expelled from the church, but he can join another if he wants to. Consequently, the churches develop a "pitch" or dogma which will appeal to the source of potential converts and the present membership.

This situation parallels what happens in the rightist camp. The churches have a common theme. Herberg says that it is the American Way of Life.[16] The rightists have the common theme of communist subversion, both internal and external, which serves as a symbolic master key that unlocks a variety of seemingly unrelated frustrations and emotions. These groups are dependent for their existence upon their ability to deal with these tensions in members and converts.

There are several ways in which the continuity of the organization can be fairly well assured. First, the organization can expand its base so that small losses in membership and allegiance will not affect it. Secondly, it can increase its control by giving token power to numerous individuals. Finally, the organizations can secure a leader with a forceful enough personality for his charisma to prevent defection. Let us see how this has worked and why some political organizations are larger and more financially stable than the Freedom Center.

As J. Allen Broyles indicates, any estimation of the membership of the Birch Society is subject to question because the society will not release any membership figures. However, as he points out, a financial report of the society for 1962 filed with the attorney general of Massachusetts listed a total income from dues as $296,326. "I would estimate that women ($12 dues per year) outnumber men ($24 dues per year) by two to one. This calculation places the total membership in 1962 at 16,463."[17] This figure of dues-paying members is much higher than that of the Freedom Center. An auditor's report on the

Center dating from July 1, 1960, to December 31, 1960, a six-month period, listed receipts from the "General Fund" as $10,169.[18] Supposedly this money came from donations, subscriptions, and pledges. The Center's total mailing list numbered about 6,000 names which were classified into those people who were "actives," i.e., those who gave time or money to the Center, and those who merely subscribed to the paper. In Portland there were 1,000 people who could be called actives, while there were at least 800 more in the city who subscribed to the paper, *The National Eagle*. Although papers were sent to literally all parts of the United States, it is likely that there were more "subscribers" than "actives" among these names. People want to see or hear that their money is doing some good. If the figures for the total membership preserve the same ratio as those for the Portland membership (and the number of contributors is probably much lower because of the local nature of the Center's activities), there might have been 2,000 contributors. A figure of about 2,000 members who could be counted on to supply funds, and then only erratically and in small amounts, was a weak base upon which to launch a social movement which aimed at attacking many elements of the dominant society.

Billy James Hargis closes his speeches with an appeal for funds. He tells his audience that all that stands in the way of "stopping the communist menace is people who are not committed." To show commitment, one must give a contribution. Hargis sends emergency appeals to his followers, telling them the Christian Crusade is on the verge of collapsing unless funds are received immediately. Carl McIntire urges his audience to "put another radio station on the air. Let's start out right tonight, who'll give a thousand dollars?" he pleads. One man stands up. "Anybody else? Then who'll make it five hundred dollars . . . a hundred . . . fifty dollars . . . five dollars," he continues. Finally, in one evening he has raised over $2,000 from the floor in pledges. Money is needed to keep the organizations going, and one can get money by expanding the membership of the movement. We will examine in greater detail the finances of the Freedom Center, but it is clear that they did not have a broad base of support.

The other way in which an organization can increase its stability is to give token leadership to many individuals while still retaining centralized power. This has been one of the most notable tactics of the structure of the Birch Society. In the Center, no one but Walter and Rosalie Huss had any authority and there were no illusions that anybody else in the organization had any.

The John Birch Society functions by having paid coordinators supervise the numerous chapter leaders and form new chapters. Each member can become a chapter leader with little effort. But all officers are ultimately responsible to and subject to dismissal by Welch. All directives come from the Belmont office and all interpretations of "dogma" come from Welch. The reasons that Welch gives for the authoritarian structure of the society is that it prevents "communist infiltration" and divisiveness in the organization. As Broyles points out, "Among the currently proliferating right-wing groups, it is by far the best organized."[19] Huss's organization is well controlled by virtue of the fact that he relinquishes no authority. But he is not able to expand his organization because it is truly a one-man show.

The final means by which a movement can retain stability is to have a person at the head who would, by virtue of his charismatic personality, prevent defection. As we noted, Huss does not exhibit this ability.

On the other hand, Robert Welch has become a public image. He is viewed by the faithful as a dedicated man, working long hours, constantly in the vanguard of the fight against communism and continually vilified by the "liberal" press. He is viewed as the organizer of an effective and semi-secret organization that is getting things done. Yet it is not out of the question to say that people expect those who are successful to look successful. Welch does; Huss does not. Huss's followers know that he is financially unsuccessful because of the apparent poverty in which he lives and they are aware that his organization is a small one. Billy James Hargis drives an expensive car, wears expensive suits, and travels comfortably. Robert Welch also appears to his public as a successful man. Part of their charisma stems from the front that they create. The public image of Walter Huss is in strong contrast. He comes out of the basement to greet visitors in an old flannel shirt and suntans with grease on them. He explains he has been working on a broken printing press. He does this out of necessity, but it does not create among his followers the image of a powerful, successful man, of whom they should stand in awe.

Huss's lack of charisma has been examined in the light of those factors which contribute to the stability of a social movement. It was indicated that the Freedom Center did not have a broad membership base. It was implied that if there were a charismatic leader, he would be able to control his movement by a personal commitment of the followers. People have to be given a *reason* to support a movement. The ability of a leader to convince people that *he* has the answer and that *he can solve problems* is a crucial determinant of a movement's vitality.

Thus the fortunes of the Center can be expected to wax and wane as larger social issues—elections, financial crisis, wars, and so forth—press people to look for organizations that will allow them an outlet. The Center does not seem to be in the favorable position to create and sustain a movement on its own. It must capitalize on what happens, in a larger social context.

3

ORGANIZATIONAL DEVELOPMENT

A detailed examination of the growth and development of the Freedom Center will allow us to compare it with the histories of other social movements, and will reveal the interrelationship among factors of membership, leadership, and growth and decline.

ORGANIZATIONAL STRUCTURE

A description of the organizational structure of the Center will aid us in understanding its past mutations. (We are referring here to the structure as it existed at the end of 1965.) The organization was dependent for its existence on Walter and Rosalie Huss. It was, in many respects, a closed family organization. In April 1965 they had no editor for their newspaper, since the last editor, a former Bible student who went to work for a conservative radio station, had quit because he wasn't being paid, and they had nobody to do filing or research. Their lawyer was Leroy B. Skousen, the brother of W. Cleon Skousen, the former FBI agent and author of *The Naked Communist.* They had a photographer, and a political cartoonist, and James Bisel, who had formerly sold insurance, had quit his job to sell Freedom Shares full time. However, he was not able to make a living working full time for the Center, and eventually had to do it part time. The headlines and type for the paper were set by Rosalie and her son John who was then a high school student at a private Christian school in Portland. Occasionally volunteers helped with the printing. In Medford there was an office with a few volunteer helpers.

Both of the Husses worked long hours to keep the Center going. Even during a program or meeting at the Center, Mrs. Huss set up a table where she could listen while folding papers and addressing envelopes. A schematic representation of the ideal[1] and the actual organizational structure in 1965 would be as shown in Figures 1 and 2.

Note that in Figure 1 the president of the Center and his staff are subservient to the board of directors. The line of authority runs from him to his executive secretary, general manager, and editor of the paper. The executive secretary ideally handles his private correspondence and takes dictation. The general manager supervises the office staff and their activities as well as telling the treasurer what his duties are. The general editor assumes the task of coordinating the activities of the research staff, writers, and correspondents. In addition, there is a public relations director who deals with the group's lawyer, their radio programs, and public meetings. Finally, all members of this organization have their activities directed toward the general membership.

This, however, is not how things worked out. As we have noted, Walter and Rosalie Huss filled practically all of the positions. They were their own public relations department, editors, secretaries, envelope stuffers, file clerks, writers, printers, and managers. They were not really subservient to a board of directors. In fact, as indicated by the broken arrow in Figure 2, the board of directors acted only in a very limited capacity. The articles of incorporation had given Huss the life-time presidency. And all of the support came from the Huss family.

If a decision was to be made, the Husses consulted one

another rather than the directors. They lived in the Center, printed the paper, did the work, and made the decisions. It was a closed organization.

That the Center was entirely dependent on the Husses was evidenced by a mimeographed letter from Rosalie Huss in April 1965. The letter began with the headline: "Walter Huss

FIGURE 1
IDEAL ORGANIZATIONAL STRUCTURE

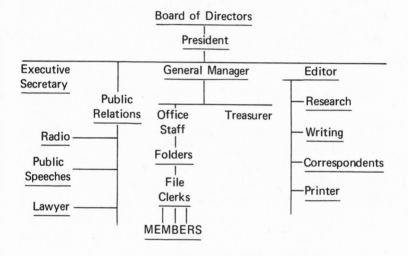

FIGURE 2
ACTUAL ORGANIZATIONAL STRUCTURE

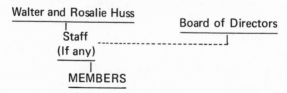

is Seriously Ill." It continued by noting that they didn't have the money to hire an assistant even though Walter had needed one for long time. "Instead of 500 hours a month, he must do less."[2] It was noted in another letter, which followed one or two weeks later, that Walter was still ill and that the publication of *The Eagle* would be held up for a short time. A visit to the Husses' home during the first part of May 1965 revealed that the work was being carried on primarily by Rosalie and her son John.

This was the situation at the conclusion of our research, but let us see what it looked like before this. We will trace the organizational growth that was rooted in the founding of the Freedom Center. In August 1955 Huss attended a meeting with the founder of the rightist Christian Anti-Communist Crusade, Dr. Fred Schwarz. This program dealt with the communist program and their "timetable" for the conquest of America. It created in Huss an "intense desire to learn more about the nature and danger of Communism."[3] The real turning point, though, came when Huss attended a special school for anti-Communists in Long Beach, California. During the week-long intensive course Huss learned "how the Communists are winning everywhere by means of stealth, subversion . . . and utilization of every known criminal device."[4] After returning, he talked to friends and other interested people and called for a meeting for December 30, 1958, which twenty-six people attended. This group, with some additions, continued to meet as the Salem Anti-Communist Clinic. Huss said that the group treated communism as a malignant disease and set out to diagnose it and look for a remedy.

Eventually Huss formed Freedom Center International, Inc., as the adult education program of the Oregon Christian Schools, Inc. The original organizational structure of the Crusade, with Huss as life-time president, was retained in the Center. The incorporation papers listed the purpose of the Crusade as:

. . . educational, dedicational, and evangelistic, and in the Christian Philosophy is committed to provide for and give education in all levels that will promote a knowledge of the Historic Christian Constitutional origin of the United States of America, to encourage the support of its Constitution, a respect for its flag, the permanence of its free enterprise system, and the defense against all its enemies, to employ all modern media in communicating ideas to reveal the nature, the danger of ideologies, systems, and enemies foreign to the perpetuation of the Historic Christian Constitutional origin of the United States, and the safeguard of religious institutions and the American Way of Life . . .[5]

The number of directors at this founding was five. They were Walter Huss, president; Arthur Wade, vice-president; William Domreis, board member in charge of solicitations; Rosalie Huss, secretary; and Jess Krater, a retired Salem contractor, treasurer. In a leaflet dated January 17, 1967, Huss described Arthur Wade.

Mr. Arthur Wade is a graduate of Iowa State College, Arizona Bible Institute, and Western Baptist Theological Seminary, an ordained minister, former principal of Portland Christian High School, present Pastor of Rose City Baptist Church, and instructor of Science and Bible at Portland Christian High School.[6]

When Huss appeared before the Portland City Council in April and May of the same year, he gave a new list of officers and staff. The board of directors consisted of Walter Huss, president; Bob Chamberlain, vice-president; Ted Swenson, secretary; Mrs. Olive Schmale, treasurer; and Walter Domreis, director. There were to be still other changes. In a *Center Fax* pamphlet (a short newsletter sent to supporters) issued for November and December 1961, Huss listed more "staff additions" to the Center. Ernest Jones had been hired to do "research and writing" and to edit the paper. In an interview in 1962, Jones said that he was a graduate of the University of Illinois in journalism. At the University of Illinois he had also been a director of student activities, and a member of the Citizen's Advisory Board for the University. For several years he had edited and published an Illinois newspaper (he was once chosen Illinois Editor of the Year), and at one time he had been director of the Illinois Press Association. He claimed to be the author of several ghost-written books, including two written for "one of the nation's leading anti-communist organization directors." (A person connected with the Anti-Communist Center indicated that Jones had worked for the Reverend Billy James Hargis.) Jones left the Center in 1962.

A news release from the Center on October 6, 1961, stated that Werner Bauer had been appointed president and founder of Technical Assistance Plan, Inc. Its purpose was to "provide spiritual aid to underprivileged countries friendly to the U.S." Bauer, too, dropped out of Center activities.[7]

Another addition was Frank A. Whetzel, president of the Lan-Lay Corporation of San Francisco. He distributed health foods and "natural" beauty products. He was to be the far-eastern representative of the Freedom Center. "A personal friend of Generalissimo and Madame Chiang-kai-shek, of Free China, Mr. Whetzel has been to many of the world's trouble spots and has acquired firsthand knowledge."[8] However, when Mrs. Huss was questioned early in 1965 about Mr. Whetzel, she said that they had not heard from him for some time, and inspection of their various publications gave no indication that he was writing any of their news stories.

Patrick D. Adam, "a language teacher and translator," was the first head of their European office. "Mr. Adam serves as head of our office in Dusseldorf, Germany. FREEDOM CENTER will supply this office constantly with the latest information available in the grim battle against atheistic communism. . . ."[9] Adam, like Whetzel, is no longer a member of the Center's staff.

The final addition listed at this time was Senator Bonhomme from the "all Negro Republic of Haiti." He was to be the Center's Caribbean representative. They supplied him with an anti-communism library, and in return, he was to correspond. "He will keep Freedom Center informed of communist movements in the Caribbean, and will draw upon Freedom Center for assistance and material to expose and oppose the enemy effectively. As funds are supplied, the FREEDOM CENTER will enable Senator Bonhomme to conduct a 30-

minute daily anti-communism broadcast to the Caribbean area from HAITI."[10] The funds were not available and Senator Bonhomme and the Center did not work together.

The organizational picture was further complicated. A combined December 1962, and January 1963, issue of the *Eagle* listed the following people as the staff members. Walter Huss was director; the office manager was Rosalie; advisor for the Youth Department was Charles Klutz, who was listed as a member of the National Advisory Board of the American Committee to Free Cuba, and was also head of the Anti-Communist Center chapter of this organization; and finally, Miss Faith Brown, head of the Research Department. These changes illustrate two things; the aspirations of the Anti-Communist Center to expand, and its difficulty in retaining help. These two things should be kept in mind as we trace the history and growth of the Center.

THE HISTORY

THE YEAR: 1959

It was in December 1958 that the Freedom Center got started in Salem, Oregon. First called the Salem Anti-Communism Clinic, it adopted the name of Freedom Crusade, as Huss put it, to "express the sense of a broad front educational function."[11] During 1959, Walter Huss traveled around the Northwest giving speeches to civic, fraternal, and religious organizations. Advertising in the papers and on radio, he called a meeting of interested anti-Communists in Portland. Only a few people attended. But Huss continued to talk and travel and by the end of the year had established two Freedom Chapters, one in Salem and one in Portland. The latter was opened in October 1959. The Freedom schools were adult leadership training schools that would "alert people to the menace of Communism," and make them "thoroughly familiar with the problem of Communism, its philosophy, its morals, its objectives and its science."[12]

The beginning of 1960 marked a period of increased activity for Walter Huss. He began publishing a small ten or twelve-page pamphlet called *Freedom Crusader*. It was originally planned to be published monthly; the original subscription form offered six subscriptions for six months at $1.00. Three editions were published in 1960. In addition to starting this publication, the Center began a daily broadcast over KWIL in Albany, Oregon. (The program has long since been discontinued.)

In an issue of the *Crusader*, Huss stated that during the month of February 1960 he traveled throughout the Northwest with two prominent rightists, John Noble and Wilmer Brown. The film, *Operation Abolition*, was shown and two "John Noble Rallies" were sponsored, one in Portland and another in Salem. According to Huss, they both drew large crowds.

In March of this same year, a "Freedom Action Conference" was held at the Portland YMCA. "Over 80 registered for the all-day Saturday conference."[13] It was also at this time that the Husses and two friends, George Whitcomb and William Dodds, attended one of Dr. Fred Schwarz's schools in San Francisco. Because of Mr. Whitcomb's interest a new Freedom Chapter was formed in Lebanon, Oregon.

April saw the second of the Anti-Communist Action Conferences, at Cascade College in Portland. A circular printed to advertise the meeting announced: "2 Double-Header Rallies!" The meeting was to feature "The Romanian Princess, Catherine Caradja." She had "escaped from her estate in Romania to tell people in the free world about the miserable life people have to live in countries under Communist Domination."[14]

Recognizing the need for circulars and other publications,

the Center bought its first press, a multilith. During this time a local Portland woman, a member of the Apostolic Faith and a charter member of the Freedom Crusade in Portland, had been seeking permanent quarters for the organization. A large two-story house in the southeast part of town was rented. This building became the Husses' new residence and the first home of the Center;[15] not however, without some guarantee of a salary, for Huss gave up his plumbing and irrigation interests in Salem and Estacada. The situation was clearly outlined in the *Freedom Crusader.*

. . . The demand upon the director has been increasing with each passing day. Some have pledged to help toward a director's salary. Additional subscriptions are needed to insure his permanent full time service. What can you do?[16]

The rally on June 27, 1960, was one of their largest gatherings and was modeled on the schools of Dr. Fred Schwarz. It ran from June 27 through July 2. A throw-away brochure announced the appearance of Herbert Philbrick, and an "airport welcome" was held for him. He came up the long ramp from one of the concourses at the Portland International Airport and was greeted by several flag-waving followers of the Center. The participants, mostly female members, were led by Mrs. Huss. The school, held at Multnomah School of the Bible, was attended by approximately 800 people, and the two audiences of the Civic Auditorium Rallies had a combined total of 4,000. Besides Herbert Philbrick, there were Dr. Fred C. Schwarz, the Australian physician; Richard Arens, the staff director for the House Committee on Un-American Activities; W. Cleon Skousen, the former FBI agent; Dr. Lyall Lush, Bible College president; Donzella Cross Boyle, a textbook writer; Dr. J. Orville Watts, economic consultant and author of *United Nations;* and Dr. Robert Allen, an assistant professor of economics from the University of Oregon. The week-long school was "climaxed" by a Saturday night Freedom Banquet at which the film *Operation Abolition* was shown.

41

The month of July witnessed an Independence Day Crusade Rally in the Portland Civic Auditorium. A former Soviet prisoner, Janis Simons, from Tacoma, Washington, told approximately 200 people about the probability of a revolt among the Soviet people. Fred Schwarz discussed the Red conquest of America. Another visiting lecturer during this month was A. Lyall Lush from Seattle Pacific College in Washington.

The *Crusader* tells us that during August "Walter Huss flew to Tulsa, Oklahoma [the home of Hargis], and Washington, D.C., making valuable contacts for the future work of the Crusade."[17] This month was highlighted in Portland by the Fourth Freedom Action Conference, another school, held from August 18 until August 22.

The rest of the year saw the same general pattern of activities. In September a rally was held in the Lebanon High School auditorium and a new daily radio broadcast was started over the local radio station there. In October the Center went on a seven-day-a-week broadcasting schedule in Ashland, a small town in the southern part of the state, over a radio station which called itself "Southern Oregon's Only Christian Radio Station." This brought the total number of radio stations on which the Center was broadcasting to seven. Other rallies and chapter meetings were held in Lebanon, Klamath Falls, in small towns scattered throughout the state, and in Portland during October and November. Purchases of materials such as recording equipment, tapes, and office supplies during this time indicated that money was coming in regularly. Another Freedom Chapter had been started in Wood Village, out of Troutdale, Oregon. In December the Center celebrated its second year with a "Birthday Rally" at the Beaver Building Auditorium in Portland. All Freedom Crusaders in the state were invited to attend the mass rally. There was to be a "top program," "a revealing message," and "birthday cake for all."[18] Miss Barbara Hartle spoke to an audience of about two hundred.

The efforts of the Center to reach a large audience are partly reflected in their expenditures for literature such as brochures, leaflets, and posters. Mrs. Huss indicated before the Portland City Council that their expenditures for literature ran just under $6,000 for the last six months of 1960. Before this same council, Huss summarized his personal activities for 1960.

We held 50 Sunday afternoon rallies, which are public meetings, with usually much publicity, in radio, press and church announcements—announcements and word of mouth; two Portland Civic Auditorium rallies; one Benson Polytechnic rally; ten rallies in cities other than where chapters are formed; 164 chapter meetings at which I lecture usually three hours; delivered speeches at 82 churches; 31 service clubs; eight out-of-State churches; ten schools; ten television appearances; 532 radio broadcasts; 200 film showings, plus the above meetings, conferences and schools, and I traveled some 38,000 miles, besides phone calls, appointments, and conferences. 8,000 miles by air . . .[19]

In 1960 Walter Huss was riding the crest of increased rightist activity in this country. Yet, with all of his activities, it is interesting to note that he was still relatively unknown to the general public. His meetings and lectures were attended, but his influence on the city of Portland and the state had not yet been felt. It was the city council hearings which finally brought him into the purview of a larger audience. We may note that many of the previous meetings had been held in churches and buildings belonging to religious organizations, such as the Multnomah School of the Bible, and had been attended by people who might have had the same world view as Huss. To such people Huss was well known; to other he was not.

THE YEAR: 1961

In January 1961 Huss flew to the east coast to make additional contacts for the Center and met with General Albert C. Wedemeyer. It was during the early part of 1961 that Huss and the Center became known to the people of Oregon. Late in 1960, he received a notice from the Portland License Bureau that the Center would have to apply for a permit if they were going to continue to solicit funds. (Huss had been asking for donations and other contributions over his radio programs and in his publications.)

It appears, from the correspondence of a city commissioner, that the impetus for requesting the Center to apply for a permit came from a housewife writing to the Better Business Bureau in March 1960, to find out "just what this organization is." It is interesting to note that the particular permit for which the Center was to apply pertained only to solicitation for business firms, door-to-door canvassing, and direct mail campaigns. Legally, it did not really apply to the Freedom Center. Nevertheless, in November 1960, Huss appeared before the Public Solicitations Commission, whose chairman was from the Better Business Bureau. According to a member of this commission there were several points that needed to be clarified and a request that the application be postponed until December was made by the Center's lawyer. On December 22, it was announced that the commission unanimously voted to recommend that the permit be granted.[20] The city council asked that the Public Solicitations Commission look further into the matter because there was some apprehension among the council members as to what some of the funds were going to be used for. The permit requested that the Center be allowed to solicit $84,000, of which $1,200 per month was to be spent for the daily radio program; $500 a month for the state-wide educational services; $1,000 a month for free literature and publication; $500 for the development of research equipment and lending library; and finally, $50,000 to develop headquarters. The objections of the commissioners are best spelled out in their own words.

Commissioner Earl: There is $50,000 [in the application] for improving headquarter facilities, which is this man's residence. . . . Then the officers of the organization—with the exception of one man, Arthur Wade—Mr. Huss fills two positions, of President and Manager. . . . Isn't that correct?

Police Lieutenant Crawford: That's right.

Commissioner Earl: That is what you call a closed corporation. . . . I just don't think it is in the best interests for us to give the stamp of approval for something as nebulous as that is—fighting Communism.

Commissioner Bean: I am not familiar with it, but I can't see giving a stamp of approval, as Commissioner Earl says, for this kind of racket. I think it is a personal proposition, and I am going to vote against it.[21]

On January 26, 1961, Leroy B. Skousen, attorney for the Freedom Center, appeared before the city council to plead their case. He told the council that this group was the only one he knew of that was spending its full time attempting to educate the public about communism. It was not, he stated, "the kind of an organization that tries to create hysteria." He described the group as very reliable and pointed out that Huss took only about $600 a month out of the income which came in. "Not very much money," he said, "for a man who has six children."[22] The group was widely accepted he continued, because they print 15,000 *Freedom Crusaders*, which go all over the world every month. The propriety of asking for $50,000 for a center in which the director would live was questioned. After more discussion the meeting was extended into February.

During January the Freedom Center's broadcast on a local conservative radio station, KPDQ, terminated. A visiting speaker for the Center, Paul Voronett, had made some questionable statements about the World Affairs Council.[23] Huss claimed he was not responsible, for he had left the city and had not made sure that the right tape was released to the station. The manager of the radio station found it necessary to make a personal retraction on the air, after Huss refused to do so. When questioned about this affair, personnel connected with the station said that Huss's attorney had recommended to him that a retraction be made if the statements were not true. Huss admitted to them that they were not true, but refused to make a public retraction because this would be "weakening to the enemy." A radio bill of $465 for January 1961 was still outstanding in 1965. Huss claimed that the station had broken its contract, and he refused to pay.

While the Solicitations Commission and city council continued to mull over the fate of the request, Walter Huss continued his request for funds. In a letter to those on the mailing list, he made it known that the Freedom Crusade was "under attack by the Communist Front Forces."

During the first part of February, Huss and his attorney again came before the city council. This time Commissioner Earl began to question Huss about his qualifications for fighting communism.

Huss: I have been a student of communism for many years as a teacher; but this concentrated effort, this national school at Long Beach, of course, was the spark that really ignited the flame in my heart. . . .

Earl: Do you know who the national secretary of the Communist party is at the present time?

Huss: He is just deceased, Eugene Dennis.

Earl: No, it is Gus Hall.

Huss: He is the president, is he not?

Earl: He is secretary of the Communist party, elected in December 1959. Dennis was president.

Huss: I believe Mr. Foster was.

Earl: He was Chairman Emeritus. Do you know how large the National Committe is?

Huss: You mean the membership of the party?

Earl: No, sir, I mean the National Committee, which is the governing body of the party in the United States.

Huss: Numerically, no. It is made up of their chain of command and organization which they have published in the publications released by the Senate Judicial Committee.

Earl: There are 60. Do you know what comprises the Politburo?

Huss: The Politburo is the name formerly used for the top, elite corps. It's been changed to Presidium, about 13 people with Nikita Khrushchev as the top.

Earl: No, there are five. . . .[24]

After this exchange, Earl produced numerous pamphlets which had the stamp on them: "Order all material in the future from the Freedom Crusade." Most of these were reprints from the *American Mercury*. Earl wanted to know if they represented the philosophy of the Center. Huss replied that "this material is for study purposes, for reference." "Yes, but it has your stamp," prompted Earl. "It is available for those people who want to read it," said Huss. Earl then found another reprint entitled: "Wanted: Earl Warren for impeachment, for giving aid and comfort to the Communist conspiracy." Commissioner Earl summed up his position by stating that:

I feel kind of ashamed that you would put out this stuff, because it certainly is neither Christian, it is not American, and certainly it is not democratic, and all I can say is that the wide dissemination of material like this gives aid and comfort to the Communist Party of the United States and to the enemies of America. . . .[25]

Huss countered by pointing out the positive aspects of the Center, indicating that numerous schools had been held, speeches had been given, and a new Freedom Crusade chapter had been opened in Medford, Oregon. This brought the total of towns with study groups to five.

Other interested persons also attended this meeting. A representative of the Portland Methodist Ministers' Association said that:

Freedom Crusade has no standing within the churches' life in this city. Indeed, their fanatical attitude is both dangerous and divisive. . . . The outcome of this Crusade . . . could be this: if all Americans start to believe that the Freedom Crusade is right in their attitude towards Russia and Red China, they might say: "Let's not sit down at the Council Chamber with them, because we cannot as Christian men and women sit down with the Devil." . . . The logical conclusion of that policy will be that we shall be decimated. . . .[26]

After exchanges between the council and other interested persons, the city council gave the problem back to the Solicitations Commission. The Solicitations Commission was instructed to conduct a full-scale investigation into the activities of the Freedom Center. At this time the members of the Solicitations Commission stated that they became "deluged with anonymous phone calls and literature with no return addresses."[27] Chairman Blyth then called the Center and asked for an explanation of several things including the details of the organizational setup. Letters also began to stream into council members' offices, some demanding that the Center be denied a permit, and some demanding that they get it. Some followers of Huss were not very happy about the outcome of the hearing, as the following officer's report from the Portland Bureau of Police indicates. The officers stated that at 7:24 A.M. they observed a Mr. Aaron M. Scott, pastor of a Pentecostal Holiness Church, standing in front of his church holding a piece of plywood. On it he had written with colored paint: "Commissioner Stanley Earl Is a Liar When He Insinuates That The Council of Churches Is Affiliated With Communists, Fascists, And Various Other Subversive Groups." When the officers talked to Mr. Scott, he said he was from the Freedom Center and that his group's application for a permit had been turned down because it had been insinuated that they were associated with Communists and fascist organizations. Mr. Scott also stated that the television portrayal of the council hearings was distorted.[28]

Walter Huss appealed to his supporters to come to his aid. He noted that the recent confusion in City Hall had "resulted in a great loss to the Freedom Crusade and [its] constituency." In the same letter he gave his version of what had happened at the council hearings.

We met with the Council and what was originally a very insignificant matter of obtaining a permit suddenly was shifted by Mr. Earl into the arena of an inflamed attack to throw the FREEDOM CRUSADE in a bad light and destroy its achievements and future in the Community. If Mr. Earl wanted to demonstrate appropriate paternal graces, he could have called me in and privately pointed out something he thought might be corrected in the organization. . . .

But instead, what Mr. Earl did was to provide the basis for sensationalism, runaway news stories, and chain reactions. Besides this, the Communists, local Communist-fronters, and Freedom Destroyers, have a basis for elation over successes which they had not been able to effect alone up to this time. THIS WE KNOW TO BE A FACT!!

What happened to myself and the FREEDOM CRUSADE in the City Hall is a classic example of how the Anti-Communism program is stifled. Communists use others as puppets while they remain in the shadows to control the strings. In Communist nations they add armed guards and severe sentences to like proceedings. . . .[29]

On about April 17 the Center's attorney asked the city council for an extension of the date for the next hearing. It was then set for May 11. It might be noted from the attorney's testimony as well as from remarks made by Center members, that there appeared to be a certain reluctance on the attorney's part to become embroiled in this controversy. Huss later mentioned that the attorney was constantly afraid of offending someone. Nevertheless, while waiting for the next hearing, the Center continued their activities. They scheduled their fifth Freedom School of Americanism in Portland's new Memorial Coliseum. It was to run from March 19 to March 26. Some people in the community began to get upset. One of the more confused complaints came from the Ladies of the Grand Army of the Republic. Their spokesman, saying that they were "direct descendants of the Veterans of the Civil War, daughters and grand-daughters of men who went forth to save this Country for our Freedom," opposed the Center's renting the Memorial Coliseum.

The Freedom Crusade has long been known as a Communistic infiltrated Organization.

The Coliseum is a Memorial to those who have served their Nation in Patriotism and Love of Country and not to those who wish to Undermine our FREEDOM and LIBERTY. . . . We are trying to keep (our country) Free from "Dictatorship."

Will you please help by using your influence by NOT allowing the Freedom Crusade or any other Pink tinged group to hold Rallies or such Meetings in the Memorial Coliseum?[30]

At the Memorial Coliseum School, faculty from their previous schools were present. High school and college students were, as usual, offered a specially reduced rate of $1.00 per day. Couples paid $15.00 to register for the school, and a single registration was $10.00. (This is less than the fee charged by Schwarz for the schools he conducts. There, a "donation" of $20.00 is asked for, or if a student wants to come for only one day he can do so for $4 to $8.)

Also during March, the students at Campbell Court, a residence for students at Multnomah College, circulated a petition asking their president to bar Centerites and John Birchers from the dormitory. The students were protesting the group's attempt to win converts in the Court. One student challenged Huss to debate, but Huss later withdrew because he claimed the student called him a "moral and social coward."[31]

The first part of April saw the name of the organization changed from Freedom Crusade, International, Inc., to Freedom Center, Inc. On April 6 the Solicitations Commission of Portland decided to recommend to the city council that the Freedom Center be granted its permit to solicit funds, if certain conditions were met. First, they wanted the articles of incorporation to specify or be amended to permit the members of the organization to vote. Secondly, they wanted to make sure that the headquarters would be used only as a headquarters, and not as the residence of any members, officers, or officials of the organization. A third restriction asked that a separate solicitation and accounting be made for the funds for operational needs and those for capital improvement. The fourth and final restriction requested that periodic reports on financial standing be made to the city auditor.[32] At this meeting, the testimony of those representing the Center was greeted by loud "Amens" from the floor. One man said that the work of the Center was going to stop atheism.

In April further problems came to the Center. A retired Methodist pastor from Gresham, Oregon, Reverend Chamberlain, filed a $35,000 libel suit against Huss. The suit concerned a letter signed by Huss, dated October 23, 1960. It asked that people write and wire the Ninth United States Circuit Court of Appeals and demand that they deny a stay of deportation for Hamish Scott MacKay and William Mackie of Portland. The letter, according to the suit, made statements which were false about the Methodist Federation for Social Action and the Committee for the Protection of the Foreign Born. Reverend Chamberlain, who was an official of both groups, asked $10,000 in general damages and $25,000 in punitive damages. However, the suit was dropped and the pastor, when questioned about the reasons for this, said that he and the organization (Methodist Federation for Social Action) decided that even if they won they would collect little, and "the suit would just give the group more publicity." Chamberlain said that he had had numerous contacts with Center people. While we were talking he had to stop constantly to answer the phone. The calls were in regard to a cancellation of a room reservation at a Portland motor motel. The reservation had to be changed to another location because the manager of the motel received many "threatening" calls when people found out that a meeting to oppose HUAC (the House Committee on Un-American Activities) was going to be held there. "These Freedom Center people scare others," he said. "They come to this sort of meeting, take notes, picket, take down license numbers, and sometimes take pictures. It really makes people nervous." When I asked him if he was sure these people were Freedom Center members he said, "No, but they act like them." I later asked Walter Huss if he had asked people to call up the motel, or if he knew of anybody who was doing so. His answer was no.

Other things happened at this time to draw the Center more and more into the public light. A Jewish temple was defaced with swastikas painted on its doors. Rabbi Rose said that the work was probably done by pranksters. "But the activities of such groups as the John Birch Society and the Freedom Crusade are partially responsible by creating an atmosphere that makes for such action."[33] Huss responded by noting that an ungentlemanlike smear campaign was being whipped up against his organization.

On Thursday, May 11, 1961, there began a five-hour televised hearing in which the city council decided not to grant the Center permission to solicit funds. The Reverend Eric L. Robinson, representating the Portland City Council of Churches, was one of those opposing Huss.

The Portland Council of Churches has been attacked quite definitely by this organization. The Council of Churches had a radio program at 12:00 noon on Saturday morning last summer, on the station known as Portland's Radio Pulpit, and it was because of the efforts of those people who are members of Freedom Crusade, putting tremendous pressures and anonymous phone calls . . . which identified them as Freedom Crusaders, that this Portland Council of Churches program was banned from the air by that station after only five Saturdays.

I would like to say, Mr. Mayor, that we asked Walter Huss, "Will you come on to one of the panels and will you take part; will you talk about these things with us?" and he refused to. . . . I know he told somebody in the station, because they told me, that he wouldn't sit in the same studio as Satan. . . . I wish we could be with these Christian brothers, but they have made it impossible.[34]

The irony in all of the hearings was unwittingly pointed out by Mayor Schrunk when he noted that the hearings did *not* affect the Center's solicitation of funds directly from its members or through mail and radio appeals. This is all they had been doing in the first place.

Huss attacked the city council in his publication and on his radio program for their "unwise" decision. The Center had grown to a membership of five thousand, he claimed, and these people were ignored in the council's decision.

Throughout the remainder of May and into June the Center continued to solicit members and grow in strength. At this time they seemed to be appealing to a number of young people in the area. It is interesting to see what sort of youth the Center attracted. In a July issue of *Center Fax* there appeared a long article entitled "The Preservation of Americanism or Bees, Ants, and Termites." It was written by two active members, Edmund A. Crump and Roger K. Gerber. In 1965 Edmund Crump was president of the National Party of America and Gerber was its secretary-general. Gerber had shaved his head and wore the silver shirt of this neo-Nazi organization. The organization, although it was not affiliated with Rockwell's group, was anti-Semitic and racist. The following is from a letter signed by Edmund Crump and dated February 9, 1965.

Dear American Friend:

It is now 11:00 P.M. and I have just returned from a lecture delivered by the Assistant Attorney-General of the State of Oregon. As you may know, he is a nigger, a Mr. Hamilton. I must confess, I am a little sick to my stomach.

Mr. Hamilton (as in Alexander, who may have owned his great grand-father) opined to the assembled Whites (there wasn't another coon in sight) that there just aren't enough negroes (I apologize for using the word) in the State of Oregon. He thought we should do all we can to attract more coons because, he predicted, non-Whites would soon rule the world, and we shouldn't be without our share. The jig praised us for our liberalism, but, as always he intimated that we haven't "ar-

53

rived" yet. He is convinced, apparently, that there are still summits of Jew-Communist race-mixing reason yet to be reached. I doubt it.

We gave him the "works," as we always do, in the question and answer period. We didn't ask any serious questions, as that would have made it seem as though we had a corpuscle of respect for the "man." Instead we asked him such questions as "What do you think of Martin Luther Koon" and "Why can't NIGGERS ever achieve subject-verb agreement?" The fleshy-nosed, scaley Jewess who had introduced him was much offended by our behavior (we laughed loudly throughout the jig's speech). She was bright enough to realize that any form of jungle life trying to put on a humanoid front would be completely deflated by laughter, especially from White men in front of a White audience. Needless to say, he was. The Jew psychology books had not prepared him for a run-in with us. In general, though, the kikes, coons and commies took the whole situation in stride, with a degree of commie-type "love" that rivaled Martin Lucifer Koon himself. I could entitle tonight's activity "One Enchanted Evening" or "How I Faced Olfactory Stultification for the Sake of the White Race." . . .[35]

I asked Walter Huss about this group and what they were doing. He said that he received their literature. There was, he thought, a problem. "They have a lot of truth in their material. They just get it mixed up with too many other things." Huss was also asked by a reporter what he thought of the group. "They don't like Jews; I don't like coffee."

The months of August and September followed the same general pattern as the previous months, with more seminars, rallies, speeches, film showings, and membership drives. The August issue of *Center Fax* already had a circulation of 17,000 but was reaching for a circulation of 100,000 by the end of 1961.[36] It was, however, being sent unsolicited to many people who were *not* sympathetic to the Center. It appeared that they had taken the names of many of the registered Republicans in the area and were distributing *Center Fax* to them. The major activity for November was the sixth "Freedom School of Americanism and Anti-Communism" held at the Memorial Coliseum from November 24 to November 26. During 1961, a total of 1724 radio broadcasts had been made by Huss. Other activities completed during 1961 were 225 film showings, 12 television appearances, 9 news conferences, 100 lectures and addresses before 40 church groups, 205 chapter meetings, 50 freedom rallies, 10 all-day seminars in new areas, 34 service and civic clubs, 25 school and college groups, and three large Americanism schools. In addition, "more than a million pieces of literature" were produced and distributed.[37] The year closed with a celebration of the Center's third birthday.

THE YEAR: 1962

In January 1962 the Freedom Center ceased publication of *Center Fax* and introduced *The American Eagle*. It outlined its objectives:

1. To defeat the advance of communism
2. To revive the struggle for freedom and to extend it to all mankind
3. To reaffirm the Christian faith in all the world[38]

Their editor, E. M. Jones, indicated that the paper was being sent to about 10,000 people by the end of the year.

It was not just the introduction of a newspaper that brought the Center to peoples' attention. There were two major incidents besides the city council hearings that caused people to be concerned. The first case, which occurred in February 1962, was the "Gus Hall Scandal." The second, to be dealt with later, was the *Northwest Review* issue. Early in the year, the Focus Club, composed of students from Reed College, invited Gus Hall, national secretary of the Communist party of the U.S.A., to speak in Portland. Shortly after the college had announced their intention to let Hall speak, the students of Oregon College of Education in Monmouth invited him, and permission was granted for him to appear on campus there. Invitations then went out from other schools, i.e., Portland

State University, the University of Oregon, and Lewis and Clark College.

Huss and the Freedom Center were opposed to Gus Hall's appearance. Freedom Center printed and circulated thousands of circulars that urged "Stop Gus Hall." The leaflets called for people to "write, wire, telephone, go in person" and protest the appearance of Gus Hall and called for the dismissal of "the consistently Left-Wing Arthur Flemming as President of the University." Over a hundred letters as well as numerous phone calls and telegrams were received by Flemming.

From a content analysis of all the letters written to Flemming, it appeared that there were three basic reasons why people were protesting. 1) They saw Gus Hall as representing the atheistic philosophy of communism; 2) They saw Hall's appearance as an attack on the American Way of Life and what people "love"; and 3) they saw Hall as a criminal who had no business speaking at a state college. There were of course multiple reasons listed in the letters received, but an analysis of the main themes of the letters received by President Flemming indicated that only 9 out of 120 letters appealed to religion as a reason, whereas 43 out of 120 addressed themselves to the American Way of Life theme, and 68 out of 120 to the "criminality" of Hall.

What kind of letters did Centerites send? By comparing the names on the letters with those on the mailing list of the Center we find that only six people from the Center wrote letters. This does not mean that people were not stimulated by the Center's activities to write letters, but that those directly connected with the Center in Portland did not write. Of those from Portland who did write, *all* addressed themselves to the religious implications of Hall's appearance. Let us examine some of these responses to see more clearly the pattern they fall into.[39]

1. Religious Reasons

You are not a truly born-again Christian, or your soul would flinch at the very thought of bringing a person who hates your

Lord in contact with the students that he might poison them with his satanic venum. We pray that you will begin seeking the Lord Jesus Christ with all your heart through prayer and study of His word, and your eyes will be opened to many evils surrounding us these last days.

2. American Way of Life

We plead with you as one patriot and lover of our American Way of life to another, that you reconsider your decision, to allow this one the privilege of using our dearly bought liberties to take away the very precious heritage from us by influencing your impressionable youth. . . .

3. Criminality of the Act

Freedom of speech is fine! We all approve of that. Let it be used for and by those of us who do approve of it. Certainly communists cannot fall in this category. . . . He is an avowed enemy of our government and should not be allowed to speak.

The responses, then, were varied, but those from the few identifiable members of the Center dealt with a religious theme. This is not surprising for, as we will see, religion permeates all of the philosophy of the Freedom Center.

The March activities of the Freedom Center continued to center around the Gus Hall issue. In speeches and radio broadcasts, Huss called for a review of higher education in the state. Besides attacking the presidents of the various colleges involved in the issue, he called for the dismissal of the chairman of the State Board of Higher Education.

It was announced in the March issue of the *Eagle* that the Board of Trustees of the Northwest Education Corporation in Seattle had voted to suspend publication of their anti-Communist newspaper, *The Northwest Sentinel,* and to merge it with *The American Eagle.* This was an important move for the Center, for it gave them the national mailing list of the *Sentinel,* and it meant that the paper would be sent to all states. So when the Center stated that they had national response, it did not necessarily mean that these people were independently attracted to the Center; many of them simply got the *Eagle* instead of the *Sentinel*. *The Eagle* eventually became *The National Eagle* because a white citizen's council in Kentucky had registered the name of *The American Eagle* for their use.

Because of the extremely crowded conditions at the previous headquarters the Freedom Center leased the former State Grange headquarters building in May. There were other pressures besides space that speeded the moving. The previous headquarters were located in a residential neighborhood and there were complaints from the neighbors. It was decided by the city that the Center could not run a "printing business" in that area, and would have to look for other quarters.

Another important event took place in May. From June 1960, until May 1962, the Center had been allowed to mail its publications at a reduced rate. This was because they claimed to be a non-profit, tax exempt, religious and educational organization. The Portland Post Office, in response to a request, examined this situation and revoked the third-class non-profit permit on the grounds that the material mailed out was not "of a religious nature." Before revocation of the permit, the Freedom Center mailings averaged over 9,000 pieces a month.[40]

During the month of May, Huss continued to speak out against the previous appearance of Gus Hall in Oregon. He went to Oregon College of Education at Monmouth, where he was invited to air his views on the subject. During his speech he began to criticize the acting administrator of the college, Ellis Stebbins, because he had allowed Hall to appear on campus. This brought the moderator of the discussion to his feet, saying that he would not permit Huss to criticize someone who was not there to defend himself, and thereby ended the talk.

Over the year there was a tapering off of response to the programs. A June meeting at the Freedom Center drew only about sixty people. Attendance at seminars and Freedom schools was beginning to drop. The call went out for more volunteers, more participants, more members. The Center continued to try to expand their program as the following announcement from the *Eagle* indicates.

CALLING THOSE WHO BELIEVE IN PRAYER

Every hour, every day, someone is needed in the Freedom Center Prayer Chapel to pray for America, for world peace, for the captive nations, for our enemies, for deliverance—for Freedom Center. Won't you volunteer to devote at least one hour a week in our chapel, to keep an endless chain of prayer to our God in the name of Jesus Christ?[41]

I visited the Center several times during the month of June and July and it was usually empty except for the Husses.

In July they acquired an old building which they described as suitable permanent quarters for the organization. Through their paper, phone calls, and meetings, they asked if anybody had property in Portland which they would make available for this building, as it had to be moved. No one responded. The Center tried anti-Communist "schools." In August the Center sponsored Dr. Mark Fakkema, who was to lead a school in Moral Training. The response to the school was disheartening for the Husses.

In September the *Eagle* announced a drive to publish the paper on a weekly basis. This drive never succeeded. People had once faithfully attended all meetings and contributed both in terms of help and money to the programs. Now the Center was attempting to accelerate its program with the assumption that public interest would increase. The Center's attempt at rapid expansion had failed, as evidenced by pleas made by Huss to his followers. A form letter circulated by Huss in September gave his views of why this was happening.

Since the communist-inspired smear attack against the Freedom Center in 1960, income dropped sharply below expenses. *Following the Moscow directive against anti-Communist organizations, our Center was AMONG THE FIRST TO BE AT-TACKED.* Since then, the vicious, untruthful and treasonable smears have been directed against the effective anti-communist leadership including Dr. Fred Schwarz and Billy James Hargis, and others.

TODAY, as a consequence, the CENTER HAS ACCUMULATED A DEFICIT OF $10,977, which is increasing monthly. This, of course, can not be allowed to continue.

As an emergency measure, and to insure stability financially during the next 12 months, the BOARD OF DIRECTORS calls upon each and every individual friend and supporter of the Freedom Center to make *an immediate sacrificial cash gift and a sacrificial monthly pledge OVER AND ABOVE WHAT IS NOW BEING CONTRIBUTED.* Only in this way can the Freedom Center continue to oppose communism with honor. . . .

In order to pay current bills each month and at the same time retire indebtedness in an orderly and satisfactory manner, the Freedom Center requires approximately $1,500 per month over and above what is now received. If each and every friend and supporter will increase his or her contribution each month as much as possible, the Board of Directors is convinced a full year of operation will be assured the Center WITHOUT THE NECESSITY OF FREQUENT CRISIS APPEALS.[42]

It would appear that this first appeal was not sufficient, for additional ones followed throughout the year. Huss had said that the March edition of the paper would be read by 125,000 in the Northwest, and then modified his claim to advertisers in the September issue of the *Eagle* by saying that 50,000 American buyers could be reached through advertisement in the *Eagle.*[43] In October the Center attempted to bolster their funds by soliciting job printing.

The Center broke into the headlines and editorial columns of the local newspaper during October because of their opposition to UNICEF, the United Nations International Children's Emergency Fund. Circulating a leaflet prior to Halloween, they urged the local citizens to "Watch Out For The Trick In The Hallowe'en Trick Or Treat Program." They suggested that when the children came soliciting for the fund on Halloween they should be given one of the Center's pamphlets which "exposed" UNICEF, instead of money.

During December there was a "For Cuba Rally" attended by approximately 100 Center members. The Center's fourth birthday was also celebrated with a cake made in the form of a Free Cuba flag. The entire year witnessed increasing financial indebtedness and other organizational difficulties. The name of their editor, E. M. Jones, disappeared from the masthead of the paper after the September edition of the *Eagle*. (Various members of the Center claim that he left because the Center was experiencing difficulties in meeting his salary, and because he got to do little of the actual "editing" of the paper. Although he had been hired to fill the position of researcher and writer he had become primarily a printer.)

Another indication that things were not as good as they had been at the beginning of the year was that the Center no longer published the year's results of activities accomplished. Instead of an increase in activities, there was a decline. In mid-1961 Huss was heard on six radio stations, but early in 1962 the radio programs were dropped. They did not resume until February 1963 when he began a program on a radio station (KLIQ) that featured the program of C. W. Burpo, Carl McIntire, and Life Line. Huss's broadcast was a seven-day-a-week, fifteen-minute program Monday through Saturday with a half-hour program on Sundays, coming directly from the Center. It was eventually dropped.

THE YEAR: 1963

This same pattern of decreasing activity continued into 1963. Only five issues of the *Eagle* were published in 1963, and there was no refund for those who had expected twelve issues.

The call went out in January for office equipment, filing folders, and filing cabinets. Two years after the call, the Center was still cluttered with newspapers, clippings, reports, notes, etc., stuffed into paper boxes stacked one on the other.

In February and March the Center was concerned with a "Washington Report" coming from the office of Congressman James B. Utt. This report became the basis of what a major television network termed "a fantastic rumor" which swept through all rightist organizations. (The sequence of events leading up to this rumor and the course that it took was the subject of a CBS documentary entitled, "Operation Water Moccasin.") Congressman Utt reported that maneuvers would be held in Georgia, including ". . . the participation of sixteen foreign allied nations and involving guerrilla warfare, psychological warfare, and counter-insurgency. . . ."

Then came the part that had been credited with starting the rumors.

We do not know whether African troops will be involved or not, but we do know that there is a large contingent of barefooted Africans that have been moved into Cuba for training in guerrilla warfare. . . .[44]

C. W. Burpo, the "Angry American" of Mesa, Arizona, spread the warning.[45] Myron C. Fagan, an anti-Semite, added to the rumor through his Cinema Educational Guild. A map was distributed, which showed how the United States would be policed by various world governments. The Irish would police the west coast, the Belgians the Midwest, the Colombians and Venezuelans the Northeast, while Russia would govern all of the South. Other rumors circulated because of Congressman Utt's newsletter. For example, it was said that thousands of barefooted African savages with rings in their ears were training in the swamps of Georgia for an invasion of the United States. The entire country was being prepared for a takeover by the United Nations. The Center was concerned about what was happening in Georgia and devoted several pages in an edition of the *Eagle* to the problem, and then printed and circulated booklets with the information.

In April the Center made an appeal asking the "future leaders of America" to participate in the Center's entry in the

1963 Rose Festival floral parade as they had in 1961. The response was insufficient and the Center did not have a float in the parade.

In May the principal activity of the Center was "documenting" a case against the NAACP and the Negro movement in the United States. The documentation began by reproducing the NAACP's Christmas Seal Campaign letter. Penciled in the body of the letter and reproduced were the following notations. After the name of Walter White, the executive secretary, were the words: "Married To A White Woman." Following the name of Lena Horne, who signed the letter, was the notation: "Married To A White Man." It was also pointed out to readers that "The Commie Press Always Boosts NAACP."[46]

In June the Center found a new headquarters and vacated their old building. Mrs. Huss said that the rent for the old location, the Oregon Grange building, was too high, and the fact that they were not able to live in it increased their overhead. The Center obtained an old building which had once housed civil defense headquarters during World War II. In a letter stamped "URGENT" the members were requested to donate money for the down payment to purchase the property. July and August were devoted primarily to moving. It was during this time that the Center acquired additional printing equipment from a printing shop that had gone out of business.

In September Huss staged a series of meetings throughout the Northwest and appeared with Max Rafferty, Karl Prussion, and Kenneth Goff. In October the *Eagle* published the Center's last paper for the year. Walter Huss filed a preliminary notice that he intended to run for Congress as a Republican candidate for the House seat held by Edith Green. During November the Center carried on its crusade, as in the previous year, against UNICEF. This time they warned people not to purchase UNICEF Christmas cards and offered, for five cents, a post card to send one's friends which read: Please Don't Send Me A UNICEF Card." Their brochures and post cards stated that "in 1961, UNICEF allocated a total of $1,536,109.46 to communist Red China—and UNICEF gave that money to the communist government to spend as it wished." As an editorial in the *Oregon Journal* pointed out with headlines such as "Shameful Attacks on UNICEF," this was not true.[47] On December 30, the Center celebrated its fifth birthday, "fighting Communist subversion."

THE YEAR: 1964

In 1964 the Freedom Center bounced back into the news with the national elections and the help of an event at the University of Oregon. Before these two "outside" events occurred the Center appeared to be losing support. This was evidenced in their frequent and urgent appeals for money and volunteers. Also, there was a severe drop in attendance at their rallies and seminars in the city. With the new focus of the elections, and what we will call the *Northwest Review* scandal, an upsurge in support occurred.

Activities in March saw preparations for Huss's campaign, and in April he outlined his bid for a house seat in a press release to the city's papers.[48] He was one of four candidates for the Republican nomination for 3rd District U.S. representative. He had served as a Republican precinct committeeman and was one of the conservative leaders who that year had dominated the Multnomah County Republican pre-primary convention and forced through a very conservative platform which, among other things, took a strong stand against the civil rights bill. In a campaign brochure called "Huss for US" his personal platform was given.

HUSS will provide a character for clean government. The "Bobby Baker type program must be smoked out."

HUSS will work for YOU and the 3rd DISTRICT. Huss believes government is a servant not a NEW DEAL MASTER.

HUSS will work for a restored dollar value to halt inflation. A 1939 dollar purchases only 44¢ worth today.

HUSS will work to reduce government control of our industrial might, agriculture and free enterprise.

HUSS will continue to work for preservation of individual freedom through education and social-economic advancement for all.[49]

A "Huss for US in Congress Committee" was formed. One of the primary reasons for the formation of a "separate" committee was that the Center claimed to be primarily a "religious and educational organization" with a tax exempt status. Because of this they could not participate in the election. In May 1964, the second *Eagle* was published, and it noted that although Huss had lost (his three Republican opponents had a combined total of 44,486 votes), he had "pulled a strong, challenging total of 21,058 votes."

Other events occurred during May in Eugene, home of the University of Oregon. The newspapers in the state carried the story that on May 2, 1964, the Lane County Grand Jury had charged more than thirty University of Oregon students with "sexual misbehavior" involving a thirteen-year-old girl. Alone, this event probably would not have caused a state-wide furor. In May, however, Walter Huss and others read the Fall 1963 issue of *Northwest Review,* a campus literary magazine. Those who read it were, according to the *Eagle,* shocked.[50] The months of May, June, and July were taken up with hurried publishing, public meetings, letter writing, and other activities relating to the university. Whereas only two editions of the *Eagle* had been printed in the space of the previous five months, five editions were published in less than two months. The first edition in the series led off: "LID OFF UNIVERSITY Garbage, They're Printing What Isn't Fit to Print!!! At your Expense—with Arthur S. Flemming President of the University of Oregon AS A MAJOR SPONSOR." They then went on to say: "FIRST LET US ASK YOU A QUESTION: Do you consider the following fit to print at public expense by State University?" Whereupon they produced numerous portions of the poem from the *Northwest Review* headed by titles like: "There's Much More—And Much Worse!!!"[51] Immediately a committee was formed, the Committee for Improved Education, with Walter Huss as state chairman. Reproductions of the "obscene and blasphemous filth" were prepared to be sent throughout the state.[52] The Portland Post Office, however, early in June held up the mailing of Huss's material because of a question of possible obscenity. Copies of the material were sent to the United States Post Office's general counsel in Washington, D.C., who ruled that the material could be sent because it was a "comment" on obscene material. A reprint entitled, "Is God Dung—The Crablouse God?" began to be circulated.

Yet another event occurred at the University of Oregon which gave the Center and the Committee for Improved Education more material. Huss found out that in February the Student Union Board had sponsored a film program presented by Gerd Stern. The films presented were *The Verbal American Landscape, Take Two* and *Y*. The films showed several close-ups of female anatomy and were accompanied by "passionate moaning and groaning," according to the *Eagle*.[53]

These three events, the film showing, the *Northwest Review*, and the County grand jury's charge against thirty students, all added up to the following analysis offered by the Center. (See Figure 3.)

On July 10 Huss traveled to Medford where the Committee for Improved Education was greeted by an editorial in the local paper entitled "Whoop It Up."

Against sin?
Believe you know what other people should be allowed, or not allowed, to read?
Believe our campuses are infiltrated by dirty Commies?
Think that anyone who has a different view than yours concerning the Deity is a blasphemer and ought to be put in his place?
Think that dirty words in a little magazine should be reproduced thousands of times to "shock" everybody?

If so, there's a meeting here for you tonight. . . .[54]

It's Happening At The University Of Oregon

IF YOUNG PEOPLE CAN BE <u>PERVERTED</u>--

THEY CAN ALSO BE <u>SUBVERTED</u> !

OBSCENE, SACRILIGIOUS, PORNOGRAPHIC, AND MARXIST MATERIAL, GIVEN WIDE ENOUGH DISTRIBUTION AMONG YOUTH,
WILL BOTH <u>PERVERT</u> AND <u>SUBVERT</u> !

THE AVERAGE CITIZEN IN OREGON SIMPLY DOES NOT REALIZE WHAT IS GOING ON UNDER HIS NOSE.

He -- or she -- can't know, for most newspapers, television stations, and radio stations conceal the truth, and fabricate deceit.

THE MODERATES AND THE LIBERALS THINK THAT'S THE THING TO DO -- CONCEAL TRUTH FROM THE PEOPLE, AND SUPPLY THEM WITH DECEIT INSTEAD.

Those who know the truth and want to inform the people find the going very difficult--and funds for doing so sadly lacking.

MAJOR SCANDAL AT THE UNIVERSITY OF OREGON IS OBVIOUS--BUT WITH YOUR HELP AND SUPPORT IT CAN BE STOPPED !!

OBSCENE MATERIAL has been published at the University of Oregon, extensively, and at public expense.

PORNOGRAPHIC motion pictures have been shown to mixed student audiences in the student union building.

MARXIST anti-American ideologies, are given unlimited distribution, with little or no press freedom at the University for American and Christian material.

SEX PERVERSION has been so rampant that even the newspapers have given that some publicity.

THIS IS THE TIME for the right kind of publicity. The only way the true facts can be gotten to the people of Oregon extensively enough is to buy space in the newspapers, buy coverage over television, and to buy time over radio stations. This must be done quickly--and if it is accomplished, I am confident that the voice of the people will be heard and heeded.

WILL YOU HELP SO THAT THE DISGRACEFUL MESS AT OUR STATE UNIVERSITY MAY BE CLEARED UP, AND THOSE RESPONSIBLE FOR IT CLEANED OUT ?

ANY SUM, LARGE OR SMALL, WILL HELP. MAKE YOUR CHECK PAYABLE TO:
COMMITTEE FOR IMPROVED EDUCATION
Walter Huss, State Chairman
P. O. BOX 3905 - Portland, Ore. 97208
Additional information and material may be obtained at: 2230 S. E. Morrison, Portland, or call 234-8493

HELP SPREAD THE WORD TO ALL THE PEOPLE !

Source: "Is God . . . Dung—The Crablouse God?," Committee for Improved Education (Portland, Oregon, about July 1964)

HEAR
5 Speakers

TELL OF OBSCENE AND SCANDALOUS CONDITIONS AT OUR UNIVERSITY OF OREGON

Friday, July 17th

8 p.m.

Emily's Restaurant

HEAR ABOUT THE NORTHWEST REVIEW AND ABOUT THE PORNOGRAPHIC FILMS

WALTER HUSS, Dir. Freedom Center
FLORENCE REED COOK, Legal Voters Eugene
CLARE DONISON, Oregon State Grange
MRS. MARTHA PEARSON, Mother of U O Student
STANFORD BETTIS, Writer, U O Student
Sponsored By:
COMMITTEE FOR IMPROVED EDUCATION

Walter Huss, State Chairman
2230 S.E. Morrison, Portland, Oregon 97214
Ph. 234-8493

TO LEARN WHAT IS GOING ON AT THE U OF O AND WHAT TO DO ABOUT IT---ATTEND THIS MEETING
Literature Available at Meeting

Source: *Brookings-Harbor Pilot*, advertisement (Brookings Harbor, Oregon, July 19, 1964).

Because of the editor's attack on Huss's meeting, the Center circulated material to the advertisers of the newspaper, advising an examination of its policies, the implication being that they should stop advertising in the *Medford Mail Tribune.* Huss's appeal had no success.

The committee traveled to another community where an advertisement that they had placed previously stated that they would speak on "obscene and scandalous conditions" at the university. (See Figure 4.)

Huss continued to tour the state, but there was dissension within the Committee for Improved Education. Walter Huss wanted to schedule a meeting in Eugene and asked me to contact Florence Reed Cook, who had been appearing with him in some of the meetings. When Mrs. Cook was contacted by phone she stated: "I don't want anything to do with Huss and the Freedom Center. I want to deal with facts. That's all, facts. Huss is too emotional. I don't want the meeting to open and close with prayers. And besides, he is always taking up an 'offering.' " Mrs. Cook was asked why she didn't wish to work with Walter Huss when she was allowing him to distribute the "documentation" she had prepared on the events at the university. She exploded, saying, "I didn't give him any permission to reproduce that. I suppose he is charging for it too!" (The booklet could be ordered from the Center for twenty cents.)

With the coming of August, however, preparations for the Goldwater campaign became more intense, and there was less activity in terms of the *Northwest Review* scandal. During August, as one of the Center members reported, Huss had decided that although he had been defeated in the May primary he would run as an independent. "I didn't give him any money, though, because he said to a group of us that he knew God wanted him to run. I think he should have taken a vote. Besides most people didn't give any money when he passed around the hat, so I don't think they believed him." During this time the Center had formed the Oregon Citizens for Goldwater-Miller Committee. The Republican party denounced the Center's setting up a separate committee. The Center said it was necessary because they wanted to concentrate their efforts on getting Goldwater elected, and did not want to bother with the other Republicans who were running for office.

This campaign did several things for the Center. It increased their financial support, because there were other people concerned only with Goldwater's victory, and who thus contributed to the Center. It also increased the number of people who became involved in the Center. Another reason for the added financial support was that the Center appeared to some people as "legitimate" as the Central Committee of the Republican party. At this time, there was a feeling among some conservatives that anybody working for the election of Goldwater was to be commended and supported. People stopped at the Center on their way past the building to give a contribution. Many people were drawn into the Center who probably would not have come under ordinary circumstances. Several local physicians as well as other professionals were giving their money and time to the Center.

The activities of the Center increased and they were able to coordinate the activities of people because there was a definite and definable goal that they were working for—the election of Goldwater. This represented an entirely different situation from a continual "fight against communism." The people had needed a definite goal toward which to work. Now the Center was busy, people were coming and going, the printing presses were running continuously. Literally thousands of pieces of literature were turned out and distributed.

With November came the defeat of Senator Goldwater. With money coming in the hopes of the Center had gone up. They saw possibilities of making the *Eagle* a weekly paper, of opening branch offices in several other cities, and increasing their public support. Working on the assumption that support would continue, they tried to expand the physical facilities of the Center. The available capital was not used, then, to establish a sound financial base. By early December the number of people coming to the Center had dropped off dramatically. One woman voiced the plight of many when she said: "We worked so hard, so very hard. I just can't bring myself to get out and work again. I know I should, but I'm so discouraged." With the fall-off in attendance, there was a drop in contributions. A new plan was introduced to bring in funds. Freedom Shares would be sold. A letter dated Christmas 1964, explained.

You, as many others . . . worked hard in the past election, and now you wonder—what can we do?

Here is the 1965 SHARING FOR FREEDOM program for the local level that offers you just the opportunity you have been waiting for!!

1. To expand the Conservative EAGLE. . . .
2. To enlarge the research center and class instruction program.
3. To widen the conservative broadcasting outreach.
4. To organize the Freedom Corps—Youth and adults alike —in constructive activity to keep America "One Nation Under God."
5. To expand the conservative speaker's bureau.
6. To use music, literature, and entertainment media as tools for the cause of freedom.

Instead of waiting just 1 month before election to work for our country—let us unite NOW to inform, convince, and organize our forces. . . .

But how much will all this . . . cost?—The unbelievably low amount of just 10¢ per day—just the price of a cup of coffee. . . . Many people are taking several shares. . . . Select the number of shares you want at just 10¢ per day ($3.00 per month) and send in the enclosed application right away. . . .[55]

But the campaign for funds was not successful. With the end of 1964, the Center witnessed its sixth year of being "on guard for America." This time there was no rally. Their staff in Portland consisted of the Husses, a part-time newspaper editor, one or two volunteers who helped occasionally, and the person who was responsible for selling Freedom Shares.

THE YEAR: 1965

With the beginning of the year, the Center planned to publish two papers, an *Eagle* for Medford, Oregon, and one for Portland. The Medford paper was to be published in Portland to eliminate the cost of installing local printing presses. It would have the same insert as the Portland paper but would have a different cover that would deal specifically with local issues. It was planned to do essentially the same thing for the eastern and western parts of the state—establish local offices that would do reporting, take pictures, and run surveys on local issues and then send the material to Portland where it would be printed.

At the beginning of the year a few rallies and meetings were held, but these were poorly attended. Most of Huss's time was taken up with trying to turn out two papers. Lacking reporters and distributors in the southern part of the state, he hurried back and forth trying to cover the events himself. The material in both papers soon ceased to be original work and prepared material from other rightist organizations and columns was used.

1965 saw a continued falling away of support, and soon the Husses were doing literally all of the work in the Center. The decline was hastened partly by Walter Huss's collapse from physical exhaustion during the spring. The radio broadcast was dropped, the publication of the newspaper stopped, and speeches were cancelled. Most of the work was being carried on by Mrs. Huss and her son. The organization was not large enough and did not have sufficient financial or organizational stability to carry on without Walter Huss. The only solution in the face of Huss's illness was to curtail activity.

The situation of the Center and the impact of its activities during this period is best summed up in the words of one reporter.

Huss failed to get his permit [to solicit funds], failed to block Gus Hall's appearances, failed to block the NAACP permit,

72

failed to get Flemming fired and failed to win the congressional nomination. . . .

Organizations like the Freedom Center depend to a great extent for their success and failure on situations that are beyond their control. The Goldwater-Miller campaign gave them an impetus for growth, as did the events at the University of Oregon. Another thing that should be clear from this brief and condensed history of the organization is that its appeal has been to the widest range of possible interests, although this range is, of course, restricted to a particular end of the socio-political spectrum. It had programs that would have drawn in traditional anti-Communists. It had programs for those ethnic groups who had fled from communist-controlled countries after the end of World War II. It devised programs that were supposed to appeal specifically to young people; and, of course, programs for the elderly. The issues covered in its publications covered taxes, governmental bureaucracies, the increased cost of living expenses, fears of ethnic organizations such as the NAACP, and so forth. The activities that were available for people ran from stuffing envelopes, going door-to-door, or pasting artificial flowers on a float for the annual floral parade. In the following chapters, we will detail the significance of offering people a smorgasbord of ideologies and activities. In the face of what would appear to be utter defeat of goals and purposes, the Center continued its activities—even if on a minor scale. What kind of a group can do this? The next chapter seeks to explore that question.

4

WHAT IS THE FREEDOM CENTER?

Rudolf Heberle gives as the main criterion of a social movement its attempt to "bring about fundamental changes in the social order, especially in the basic institutions of property and labor relationships."[1] In some respects the Freedom Center conforms closely to this qualification, in other ways it does not. Many rightist philosophies offer no solution for the problems with which they are concerned. They are primarily negative in the sense that they attack governmental programs and existing social conditions without advancing legitimate alternatives. However, in the presidential election of 1964, most of the rightist leaders expressed the hope that Goldwater's election would make "new changes in the social order." Manifest in all rightist publications was the belief that Goldwater represented and understood their programs and would solve their problems. For a period of time, Goldwater's campaign became the main focus of many rightist groups as well as the Freedom Center.

As we noted previously, Huss also ran in 1964. He campaigned for the Republican nomination for United States representative. His platform outlined some of the changes he would have made if elected, such as working for the restored dollar and reduction of government control.

Thus there was some attempt among Centerites, through support of Goldwater and Huss, to change the social order. The Center has also been concerned with changing the social order in other ways. But they are concerned with change in order to arrest forward movement, not to facilitate it. They have the notion that America has descended from a Golden Age, from a past when, for Centerites, "freedom flourished and all were good, loyal Americans." The historical cycle must not be allowed to run its course, for what lies at the end is "the communist takeover." They published the *Eagle* to help alert the public to this menace. Most writers on social movements have dealt with the movement which advocates a dramatic change in governmental structures so that a new age can be reached in which the followers and faithful will receive their just rewards. Theorists have not generally dealt with social movements that wish to retard change and go back to the past.

MODEL FOR A SOCIAL MOVEMENT

To what sort of a pattern does a social movement, whether its ideology is of a positive or negative nature, conform? Jerome Davis, in *Contemporary Social Movements,* traces the cycle of change through which he sees movements progressing.

Every social movement tends to traverse a cycle of change. First of all, there arises a tangible need, and some individual or group begins to voice this need more or less publicly. Second, propaganda and agitation result. Third, there follows a growing consciousness of this need in a small or large group. Fourth, they organize. Fifth, concerted action and strong leadership develop and new converts are won. Sixth, if the movement is successful it becomes institutionalized—becomes the pattern of the majority, and group control sets in. Any

75

one who does not conform to the new pattern or code is disciplined. Seventh, eventually bureaucracy, inflexibility, and reaction become dominant.[2]

How does the Center conform to this particular pattern? First, as Davis notes, there must arise a tangible need. (By implication, it is the leader or leaders who recognize the need and articulate it.) It was, according to Walter Huss, a dramatic moment for him when he attended a special school for anti-Communists in Long Beach, California. Dr. Schwarz told those present how the Communists were winning everywhere, and Huss was determined to act.

Upon returning to Salem, Huss contacted some of his close friends and other interested acquaintances and told them about the meeting. "They too," said Huss, "were deeply shocked and concerned."[3] The group met and discussed the problems involved in studying communism and analyzed how they might attack the general problem. This pattern calls for a modification of the first part of Davis's typology. After a need has been felt by some individual he will begin to talk about it with others. There then comes a period of time when the problem itself is specified, or the need is specified, and various solutions are advanced. This action takes place at the small group level. A large group has not yet become involved.

The next steps in the cycle of change given by Davis are that agitation and propaganda are the result of the expressed need; there is the growing consciousness of the need; and the group which is concerned organizes. This process was reversed in the Center. After an expression of the original need, the need was clarified in numerous discussions. For example, at this time the followers of Huss were meeting as the Salem Anti-Communist Clinic and carrying on lengthy meetings. There is, then, a nuclear organization which is present before agitation and propaganda come into play, for example, the Salem Anti-Communist Clinic. After a need is expressed and reformulated by a small group of people, they begin to proselytize. They try out their new ideology on other people. This early stage represents a "trial run" to see how other people will respond to the need. After the stages of reformulation and initial proselytizing, another reformulation may take place and then an attempt to reach a larger number of people will be made. It is at this stage that the formal organization is likely to appear.

Throughout 1959 and 1960 Huss traveled and spoke to church and civic groups about the problem of communism. In the latter part of 1960 Huss had a daily radio broadcast over a Portland radio station (KPDQ) which beamed forth

documented, irrefutable material on this subject of Communism and world conquest.[4]

The call was upon our director to give up his gainful employment in order to concentrate on the school. This he did. The overwhelming success of the school and the rapid Freedom Crusade growth proved this sacrificial step to be a wise choice.... [5]

These are examples of the phase of initial propaganda. During this time, more reformulation was taking place. Huss made numerous inconclusive generalizations about communism and subversion, and there was no attempt on his behalf to "document" his accusations.

The stage of formal organization and Davis's fifth stage of "concerted action" followed shortly on the heels of reformulation and propagandizing. In May 1960 Huss became the full-time director of the Center's activities. He gave up his plumbing and irrigation businesses and moved to a headquarters in Portland.

The stage of social action outlined by Davis found its counterpart in the Center's attempts at increased activity and dissemination of propaganda. The formal social action of the Center took the form of numerous rallies and anti-communism schools. The action was not designed to institute a new form of government or change the existing one. It was propaganda action designed to win new converts. Thus, the stage of action which Davis had envisioned for social movements may not occur in rightist groups like the Freedom Center. Their social action takes the form of increasing the number and size of programs and rallies. There is often, in addition, a modification of the original "action goal." The group may start out with the idea that they are going to change things, and then modify their goal so that tangible things can be accomplished and the converts will not desert the movement. This is one of the main reasons that such a diverse range of activities—some seemingly unrelated—are offered to converts.

The Freedom Center outlined modest programs of action to meet this need. Members were to call newspaper editors and businessmen and show them that the rightists were "influential." If a newspaper expressed anti-rightist sentiments, one should, for example, write letters to the editor or cancel his subscription. If a television program was sponsored which cast rightists in a negative light, then there must be "action."

Now, as Davis rightly indicates, if the movement is successful there will be a shift to group control and bureaucracy, and inflexibility will become part of the organizational pattern. The Freedom Center was, as we have noted, run by one person, Walter Huss. There is an inflexibility in the organizational machinery, but this is not because of bureaucracy.

Here is a modified typology, developed by examination of the Center, which is offered as a model for those movements that "fail."

1. A generalized need is realized by an individual who sees it as his duty to communicate this realization to others.

2. Others are made aware of the problem, and there is a restatement and a reformulation of the original need. Alternative solutions are advanced for this problem.

3. Others are brought into the confidence of the original group and a small group is formed which begins to

initiate plans of social action. The group becomes organized with official leaders.

4. There is an initial propaganda "experiment" in which the need is expressed in public and solutions are advanced.

5. At this time there may be a reformulation of policies and an attempt is made to reach a wider audience.

6. Social actions programs will be advanced. There will be increased propaganda efforts to win converts.

7. At this time, if the movement is successful it will, as Davis indicates, become subject to group control. If it is not successful, two things will happen:

   a. There will be a diversion of the means and goals. All activity organized by the group becomes a way of achieving the ultimate goal. So that converts will not drop out, there is an effort made to indicate to them that they are "winning the battle."

   b. It will continue to be run by one leader, or a small group. The group's activities will not be subject to control by the members.

Let us see how another conservative organization like the John Birch Society which, like the Freedom Center, has not reached its "ultimate" action goals, conforms to this pattern of development. During the height of the McCarthy era in 1952, Robert Welch was doing some independent investigation of his own. Carefully studying volumes of congressional hearings, Welch stumbled on some of the facts surrounding the death of Captain John Birch. In 1954 he published *The Life of John Birch.* This work was both a biography and a condemnation of the United States government. John Birch had, according to Welch, been murdered in cold blood by the Chinese Communists and the event was "hushed-up" by governmental agencies.[6] Other studies led Welch to his increasing discontent with the federal government. Thus, a generalized need was recognized by Welch and he decided to communicate it to others.

One of the initial things he did was to communicate his

suspicions about Eisenhower to some of his friends. These were later written up in *The Politician* and circulated among a close-knit group. He was also publishing at this time *One Man's Opinion*, later called *American Opinion*. When the society was founded in 1958, Robert Welch met with eleven interested men in Indianapolis, Indiana, and presented a list of activities to be carried out, many of which were detailed in *The Blue Book of the John Birch Society*. This phase represented the second stage outlined in our model.

The third stage, in which others are brought into the confidence of the original group, saw Welch traveling to selected cities in the United States and meeting with people who were sympathetic to the conservative cause. After others had been brought into Welch's confidence, "plans" were activated. The society was originally to be composed of a small council who would give the founder, Welch, the benefit of their advice and guidance.

The stage of initial propaganda experimentation is represented by Welch's traveling and talking to small groups. His numerous public and private publications are also an example. This need was stated in *The Blue Book*, along with reasons for beginning Birch activities in the United States.

First, because it must be our more earnest hope and goal to break out of this straightjacket woven of pretense, deception, audacity, and terror, before it completely encompasses ourselves. And secondly, because the American support of the Communist conspiracy is now the backbone of its strength, and has been for many years. If and when we can reach the point of turning just the American government from actively helping the Communist conspiracy everywhere in the world, we shall have won a most important battle in the war ahead.[7]

One plan advanced was the establishment of reading rooms with conservative literature. These reading rooms would extend the circulation of Americanist periodicals. Supporters of the society would also extend the influence and audiences of conservative announcers like Fulton Lewis, Jr. and Clarence Manion. Programs of letter-writing were to be organized. The attempt to carry out these and other prescriptions in *The Blue Book* represents the fifth and sixth phases of our modified typology. The society was trying to reach a wider audience and to structure their programs to win converts. They will always be in this stage because of the nebulous character of their goal.

In this sense, then, the society is unsuccessful. It is not able to obtain its stated goal of "preventing the American government from helping the Communist conspiracy everywhere in the world."[8] As we have noted, two things will happen if the ultimate goals of an organization are not reached. There will be a diversification of means *and* goals. What we mean by this is that numerous identifiable and obtainable goals will be introduced, as well as a variety of means to achieve the necessary ends. All of these means, however, are supposed to relate to the ultimate goal of ridding the world of communism. For instance, when the society tells its members to "Impeach Earl Warren," and to "Get US Out of the UN and the UN Out of the U.S.," means are offered to the members for accomplishing these ends. Meetings are held, letters are written and sent, phone calls are made, and organizations are infiltrated. Members have been urged to use P.T.A. groups as front organizations for "getting rid of the Red influence in our schools." A corollary of the proposition that there will be a diversification of goals is that with the diversification of goals and means to obtain these goals, comes assurance from the leader of the organization that the members are really winning the battle. One can see this technique used in a variety of groups. If the organization is attacked and vilified, this "proves" that they are getting at the Communists. Welch, in his *Bulletins*, tells his members that they belong to the most effective anti-Communist organization in the United States.

The second condition that relates to a movement's lack of success would be its continued dependence on a small leadership hierarchy or one leader. This has happened in both the John Birch Society and the Freedom Center, though for very different reasons. Welch, when he founded his organization, realized that the most effective way to achieve his purpose would be to run the society from the top down. As John Broyles pointed out, Welch was able to go down to the grass-roots level and recruit members. And he has been able to maintain his leadership.[9] Orders come directly from Welch down a rigid ladder of authority, and he, not the members, makes the decisions; he decides what activities will be carried out. It is a sound position, for there are many different motives waiting to be acted upon by individual members. Someone in a social movement must give direction to the frustrations and expectations of the members.

The Birch Society grew and maintained a fairly stable base of support. But the Center did not. Why? Welch directs the activities of the society by carefully delegating authority. Huss is not able to delegate authority to other people interested in the cause. This, it must be stressed, is one of the *primary* reasons why the Center has not expanded. As people connected with the Center have indicated: "He wants to do it all. He won't trust anybody else with the work." He will of course trust others to do "harmless" tasks like mailing materials. This is one of the reasons why the Center has failed to grow and enlarge its source of financial support and its number of members.

SECT OR CHURCH

It is evident that the Freedom Center cannot be considered a social movement, nor could it at any time of its development. Because of the religious nature of much of the rhetoric of the Center, it might be more reasonable to compare it to religious organizations and movements. The models provided for the analysis of sect and church can serve this purpose. Suffice it to say that we are not trying to fit the Center into either of these categories, but to compare them to these categories for analytic purposes so that we may better understand the internal dynamics of the Center.

H. Richard Niebuhr points out, in *The Social Sources of Denominationalism,* that over a period of time a religious sect will either die out or become a church.[10] First, the "sects" usually preach a type of asceticism that tells people to work hard and save their money. If the members of the sect practice these tenets, there will be an increase in wealth and the sect will move up the socioeconomic ladder and become middle class and "churchly." It may also draw members from the middle class "coming down" to join the sect and thus elevating it. As the sect increases in wealth, there is a greater opportunity for involvement in the larger culture. This leads to a modification of the rigid ethical and moral prescriptions laid down by the founders of the sect, and the sect appeals more and more to people of the middle classes. Another contributing factor is the second generation. The children of members must be appealed to and it is not always likely that the doctrines which appealed to their pioneer parents will appeal to them. Thus, the children's contacts with the larger social world bring a modifying influence to the social doc-: trines of the sect. Finally, with the sect moving in the direction of a "church," some of the more militant members may split from the main body and form a sect of their own. When the "radical" element is thus removed from the parent sect, it quickly progresses on its way to becoming a church, or as Niebuhr says, another "civic association."[11]

How does the Freedom Center conform to the pattern of growth that a sect will take to become a church? We will examine these processes to see whether the Center has moved in a churchly direction, and whether it will ever move in that direction. One of the conditions causing a sect to move in a church-like direction is the problem caused by the second generation. The religious sect tempers its militant social doctrine to attract youth. The Freedom Center, however, has not really had to deal with the problem of a second generation in a strict sense. The replacements that do occur in the movement do not occur because a member's child joins. Membership replacement comes from converts. When the Center was initially formed there was an attempt made to bring children of adult members and other adolescents into the movement. The activities did not, however, appeal to many, and in 1962 and 1963 there was a cessation of youth activities. Adolescents did not aid the sect's movement in a church-like direction because there were not enough potential young converts to make altering the dogma feasible.

The religious sect may also become a church because it preaches an asceticism which encourages people to save their money. The sect then moves, because the people themselves have moved up socially and economically. The Center makes great use of fundamentalist religious dogma in their publications and public speeches. Yet the asceticism which is part of their dogma is of a different sort from that which facilitates upward movement. Their dogma encourages strengthening oneself for the battle against communism by study and intensive effort. One must never rest or be idle. If one lives in an ascetic manner, it is only so he can contribute more to the cause. The type of moral dogma promulgated by the Center is not of a sort designed to elevate the members into a higher social class.

A sect may move up to a churchly position if members of the middle classes come into the sect and "pull it up." We noted that during the Goldwater-Miller campaign there were several professional people involved in Center activities. The help of these people was not, however, used to the best advantage. Two or three well-educated women were put to work addressing envelopes and stapling materials. Everyone who came to offer help was placed on the same level. There was a division of labor, but with only two levels—the people who were helping, and those who were directing. In this case, it was Walter and Rosalie Huss who gave the directions. It cannot be denied that this pattern probably accomplished the most. It did not, however, allow the people from the higher social classes to become integrated into the movement.

An impetus for church growth may be given when the more radical members of a sect decide that the sect is becoming too conciliatory in its approach to the world, and drop out to form their own sect. If this tendency exists at all in the Center, it works in the opposite direction. When the Center was first organized, and throughout 1961 and early 1962, conservatives of varying stripes were attracted to it. As the Center continued in its programs, however, it became evident that there would be no tempering of philosophy and that the Center was first and foremost a radical rightist organization. People who were once interested in, and had supported the Center, said that they just "could not agree with some of the things Walter did." Huss was invited to religious, civic, and fraternal organizations less and less frequently after the early years. There was, then, a schism in reverse. The more liberal members left the Center.

A final means by which the sect experiences an upward movement is through the accumulation of property such as buildings and equipment. The Center rented its first two headquarters and was supposed to be buying its third. Yet the tax assessor's records indicate that two years had elapsed without anyone paying any property tax on the building or grounds which the Center occupies. In addition, as noted by the Center's own publications, there were financial deficits to be overcome. In terms of sheer bulk, there has been an accumulation of property, but this does not represent an accumulation of quality materials. The furnishings of the Center are old and some are in need of repair. In short, the Center has not been able to strengthen its political position through financial gains.

In terms of the conditions laid down by Niebuhr for the movement of a sect to a church, we see that the Center has not progressed beyond the sect level. It is not unusual, though, for some sects never to make this change. This fact was pointed out by Bryan Wilson when he dealt with the problem of why some sects become churches, or in his terms "denominations," and others do not. He described four types of sects, among them the Conversionist, the Adventist, the Introversionist, and the Gnostic, of which the Conversionist was the most likely to progress in the direction of a denomination. This was due to the fact that in the Conversionist sects there was a strong emphasis on evangelism and they tried to accommodate as many groups as possible. This meant that there was not a tendency for the sect to set itself apart from the world, but to become actively integrated.[12] Now the Center wishes to convert people to its position, but they want to do it on their terms.

LIMITS TO GROWTH

There appear to be several reasons why the Center has not and will not traverse the cycle of growth experienced by certain types of religious bodies. We will examine in turn four factors which have inhibited the growth of the Center and also any possible future growth. These factors are the leadership structure, the recruitment mechanisms, the themes of the Center, and the use of religion.

LEADERSHIP STRUCTURE

We have already examined the leadership of the Center and have seen how Walter Huss will not allow others to become involved as leaders. We have also seen Huss's inability to work in a cooperative manner with others. For any organization to expand, there must be a division of labor and some delegation of authority. One complaint of people who have worked at the Center is the lack of a feeling of responsibility.

RECRUITMENT MECHANISMS

The early American revivalists held meetings to bring the uncommitted into the fold, and so has the Center. Large anti-communism schools were held, featuring prominent national speakers such as Herbert Philbrick and Dr. Schwarz. The sinful nature of the anti-Christ, communism, was dutifully exposed. People at these meetings were asked to become converts to the cause. They could help by joining the Freedom Center or forming a chapter in their own community which would allow them to carry on the battle. The Center would supply the tapes, films, and pamphlets necessary to study the communist problem. This was one means by which members were recruited.

Similar to this technique were the many one or two-day rallies held in various Oregon communities. Walter Huss would travel alone, or perhaps with another student of the problem. The general pattern which these meetings followed was, first, to have a speech telling how the "Communists are winning everywhere." Dates of the projected communist takeover in India, the Caribbean, and ultimately the United States, were given. The horrors of communist takeovers were depicted and then people were asked: "What can you do about it?" The answer put to them was "join an anti-Communist group." Organize to fight. The Center was offered as an alternative to communist world domination. People could subscribe to the *Eagle* and/or subsidize other Center projects. One of the initial ways in which people were led to the Center was through newspaper and radio advertisements.

Although it cannot be called a recruitment mechanism, unsolicited publicity does affect the size of the Center's membership. Walter Huss realizes that the television and press coverage of Center activities has done the Center more harm than good, as we can recall from the televised proceedings of the city council.

But if few members have come in from such types of recruitment, how have people become acquainted with the Center's activities? The rallies, anti-communism schools, and advertisements contribute to membership but there seems to be a more important factor at work. This is the element of friendship matrices. In other words, after a single person has become connected with the Center by attending a school or responding to a radio advertisement he will bring his friends into the movement.

There are indications that many friendship groups exist in the Center. At a small meeting, two or three people may come in together and greet other people they know. Several people may come in by themselves, but it is a rare instance if these people do not see one or two acquaintances with whom they san sit and chat. One of the more dramatic examples of these friendship matrices occurred during the second phase of the interviewing. This was the part conducted by professional interviewers, and was preceded by introductory letters. As indicated previously, this set off a chain of phone calls. People who had received the letters began to call each other to see if they had also received a letter. Members called Mrs. Huss to see why they had been contacted. "Why am I and all my friends getting these letters?" was a standard query. The importance of friendship matrices will be discussed in detail when we trace the *career* of the radical rightists in our last chapter.

CHANGING THEMES

As Niebuhr notes, in the sect's history there may come a period when the sect is no longer completely alienated from the dominant society. Its ideals and norms become similar to those of the larger society. In the Center's history, however, we find a case in which all published material, as well as radio programs, evidence an attack on the dominant society. If anywhere along the line there had been a "softening" of their ideology, we could expect to have seen them appeal to a larger number of people. But by keeping the ideological content of their themes at the same level, they restricted the number of possible converts. This fact is obviously related to Walter Huss's position. This finds its inter-connection with recruitment mechanisms, because possible members are limited to those with *pre-determined* religious and political beliefs. There is, however, a divergence of themes in terms of the things the Center attacks and "exposes." By extending their attacks into practically all areas of the larger society, they allow potential converts to channel their fears, frustrations, and aspirations in a number of directions. Let us examine some changing "attack" themes as evidenced by an examination of the *Eagle* since its beginning in January 1962 to March 1965 and other selected publications. This will also involve an examination of the Center's philosophy of the social world which as we will see is basically conspiratorial.

The first issue of the *Eagle* outlined the communist conspiracy, exposed a local paper, and told of the vicious attacks on anti-Communists. A local paper, the *Oregonian,* was attacked with the headlines: "Portland Newspaper Smears Center à la Red . . . Paper's Policy Exposed."[13] This attack occurred because the paper had questioned the ideals and motives of the Center in an editorial.

Another headline succinctly stated the Center's attitude toward the civil rights movement and Martin Luther King: "Communist-Approved Martin Luther King Welcomed by Oregon's Chief of State."[14] A look was taken at the "Smear Vocabulary Now Used Against Anti-Communists."[15] The United States government's role in current affairs was also looked into.

A State Department housecleaning is most urgent. Write your congressman. Call for an immediate investigation. Use postcards—they're quicker, to the point, and are seen by more people.[16]

This same theme found expression in their attacks on various government officials:

Basically, Mrs. Green is one of the most rabid left-wingers in the Congress. . . . (Her) voting record is consistently to the left. . . . [17]

There were special events which occurred during the

year in the state to which the Center turned its attention. One of them, as examined in the history of the Center, was the appearance of Gus Hall on various college campuses throughout the state. This issue provoked numerous demands from the Center. Members of the Center were urged to

keep a close watch upon speakers scheduled now by colleges and universities and you will observe that many of them express pro-communist and socialist views helpful to the communist conspiracy. . . . [18]

Let us continue a brief review of some of the issues to which the Center addressed themselves during the years 1962 to 1965. We have already examined many of the special circumstances such as the *Northwest Review* scandal, but we now want to examine the *Eagle* for themes which illustrate the philosophy of the Center, and then see why attention to certain themes has inhibited growth and expansion of the Center.

A dominant theme which continues to be expressed throughout the literature is the idea that the United States government and its representatives are aiding the cause of communism in one way or another.

The same hush-hush that provided Fidel Castro with the protection he needed to capture Cuba for the Reds is now giving Moscow the time to make a base for space war out of Cuba. IN BOTH INSTANCES, THIS PROTECTION WAS PROVIDED BY THE STATE DEPARTMENT.[19]

A theme that has been noticeably absent from the Center publications is that relating to the problem of fluoridation. One would expect that many of those people who oppose the fluoridation of the water supply are potential rightists and, conversely, that a rightist is likely to oppose fluoridation. This idea was given formulation when Arnold L. Green investigated the ideology of anti-fluoridation leaders. He postulated that those people who held apprehensions about the social order would be most likely to view fluoride as a poison. But what is important to note is that

. . . the fluoridation controversy is itself a surrogate issue as mediated through an ideological image that sees government and business arrayed against the essential ethical premises of American life, fluoridation is tagged with a contempt for individuality, and is emblematic of an ultimate aim to smother personal identity in a homogeneous mass. Opposition to fluoridation is an act of moral resistance.[20]

If this is indeed the case, then why do we not find the Center attacking fluoridation as an "insidious menace?" In over three years of publishing their newspaper only one article on the subject appeared and then under the rather innocuous title: "Evidence Mounts Against Fluoridation." No statement is made to the effect that it is a communist plot. All that is said is that it is difficult to control the amounts added to the water supply and that fluoride corrodes water pipes and other water equipment. Even though there are anti-fluoridationists who belong to the Center, the Center does not offer for sale any material on the subject, and does not print any article about it. This seems strange for the reason that the anti-fluoridationists might be possible converts to the Center if Green's reasoning is correct. The reason given by Huss for not dealing with this subject is that: "There just isn't enough time to do everything." The theme of anti-fluoridation, then, is not part of the Center's dogma or philosophy.[21]

Yet a theme which has found support in other rightist groups, notably the John Birch Society, "Get US out of the UN and the UN out of U.S.," is evidenced throughout the various issues of the *Eagle*.

Nearly bankrupt, the United Nation . . . expects the American people to buy millions of dollars worth of UN bonds in 1962 to enable the communists to continue such outrages against freedom as transpired in the Congo.

One of the powerful subversive movements within the United Nations is to bring about a transfer of allegiance from native land to the United Nations.[22]

Another theme that has continued to dominate Center

literature since the *Eagle* was first published is that of opposition to civil rights measures. This takes the form of a direct attack on the movement itself as well as attacks on the conduct of leaders and followers.

A headline in the *Eagle* states: "King Speaks at Highlander Commie School of Agitation."[23] Another issue warned about the evils of miscegenation:

Intermarriage of the races is a communist—not a Christian —proposal. COMMUNISM DENIES THERE IS A GOD. COMMUNISM DECLARES MAN TO BE NOTHING BUT AN ANIMAL, OR MATTER IN MOTION. IN AN EFFORT TO DEGRADE MAN INTO A STATUS OF NONENTITY, INTER-MARRIAGE IS PROPOSED. . . .[24]

Another theme which permeates the literature relates to the Center's idea that a liberal is ultimately no better than a Communist.[25]

One of the cute tricks of these left wingers is to impress upon the uninitiated that they are anti-communists—because they will say, "Practically everyone is against Communism."

But the acid test to give these liberals is—

1. Are they actively aiding the anti-communist program and helping develop an effective public and private education program?
2. Are they exposing the local Communist sympathizers and fronters?
3. Are they pointing out the infiltration processes of the subversive into all facets of society?
4. Are they working to resist the Communist Line from being promoted through school, church and other media?
5. Are they seeking to defeat Communism here and abroad?
6. Are they seeking to strengthen all the Congressional Committees and the FBI assigned to the task of coping with subversion in the U.S.A.?[26]

All movements such as peace movements, peace marches,

or any other demonstrations against the government are suspected by the Center.

"Peace and friendship" are mouthed by communists, who have anything but peace and friendship in mind, as for young people, the communists have learned from the psychiatrists that they can be brain-washed and duped into doing anything, they are using young people throughout the world for their evil purposes in the name of "peace."[27]

As far as peaceful co-existence with communist countries, the Center feels that, "It is morally wrong to pretend that your enemy is not your enemy. . . ."[28]

There are many other "themes" which are of course derivations of some of these. For example, if anyone opposes activities of the House Committee on Un-American Activities his motives are seriously questioned. If someone believed that Chiang Kai-shek should leave well enough alone and not invade Communist China this person too was suspect.

The themes presented in the Center's many publications can be condensed into a few basic propositions about the social order.

1. All aspects of internationalism are part of the Communists' plan to take over the world.
2. The anti-Communists are attacked because they are the only people preventing a communist takeover.
3. There has been a sell-out in higher government circles with many officials consciously and unconsciously aiding the communist cause.
4. Our government is turning away from the Golden Age of our heritage and subverting the truths espoused by our founding fathers.
5. Social welfare is a subversion of our American heritage and aids the communist cause.
6. There has been a breakdown in morals which aids the communist conspiracy.

Combined, these themes present a belief in a conspiracy theory of history. The present world state is seen as having been brought on by a combination of factors: internal sub-version, apathy, sellouts in high places, and a breakdown in morals. If incomes are not adequate, it is because too many people are living off welfare. For elderly people, who have witnessed changes without understanding them, an explanation is finally offered.

What attraction, finally, do these themes hold for people, and what contribution have they made to the Center's tendency to remain a sect? There are, obviously, two tendencies at work in the above themes. One tendency is to draw people in because of the relative divergence of these themes. The other is to drive people away because of the basic nature of the themes.

But, as we noted, there were four things that must be examined together to understand why the Center has remained small—leadership, recruitment mechanisms, themes, and uses of religion. If the themes represent an ideology which holds a potential attraction for a number of people, then we must examine religion in conjunction with this. For the type of religion which the Center makes use of is consistently reflected in the themes which are chosen and this limits the membership of the Center.

USE OF RELIGION

When we observed Walter Huss's occupational background, we took special note of his religious background for it is the combination of fundamentalist religious dogma with a conspiracy theory of history which characterizes the Freedom Center. The use of religion that the Center evidences is a part of their philosophy and the two—ideology and religion —cannot be separated.

A brief examination of quotations from Center publications will indicate the nature of the religion employed. When the Center reacted to a criticism of their projected entry in the 1961 Grand Floral Parade in Portland, Oregon, they had this to say:

We told a beautiful historical story. . . . This brings one closer to the great people of our history. . . . Since history is in reality "His-Story" and "the self-revelation of God in the events of on-going time in a world that is sin-perverted and Christ-redeemed."—It is very easy to detect that the history of America is Providence in action.[29]

If American history is guided by God's hand so too is the destiny of the Center. "Freedom Crusade has grown with real victory this year. It is the Lord's doings and to him be the glory. . . .[30]

A letter soliciting funds states that the Center's work is God's work and that Huss knows that the people will come through.

I am convinced . . . that our work is of God and that you will see us through. . . . I pray for you, and God knows if we have accomplished any good . . . you deserve much credit and appreciation.[31]

It is not unusual that the Center should take this position if we recall the purposes that were outlined in the original Articles of Incorporation.

The purpose of this Corporation is educational, dedicational, and evangelistic, and in the Christian Philosophy is committed to provide for and give education in all levels that will promote a knowledge of the Historic Christian Constitutional origin of the United States of America.[32]

The fight against communism, then, becomes a moral battle.

This is a battle against godless powers, against the rulers of the darkness of this world, against spiritual wickedness in high places.[33]

The relationship between being a good Christian and

being an anti-Communist was spelled out in more detail in an issue of the *Eagle* which told that communism is an enemy of Jesus Christ, of the United States, and of the individual soul.

The ideology of the Center represents a unique position. *By viewing a portion of American history as the unfolding of a manifest destiny, they have arrived at the position that any attacks upon this "heritage" are religious attacks. The American Way of Life becomes a sacred way of life which represents the forces of good in the battle with "godless and atheistic Communism."*

All of the activities of the Communists, or any activities which "aid and give comfort" to the communist cause, are therefore atheistic. The Center sees itself as an "arm of Jesus Christ" and any attacks on the Center are attacks from atheists and/or Communists. "The liberals, Socialists, Communists and fellow-travelers" who make up the perceived opposition of the Center and other rightist organizations are on the side of evil. With this position, arbitration and discussion of different political philosophies is impossible for, as Huss has said, "Who can sit with the Devil?"

The Center is a militant, fundamentalistic rightist organization. As part of this fundamentalistic stance there comes a chiliastic attitude. The world is evil but it can be good. Yet it cannot be both. There cannot be Communism *and* Capitalism. There must only be one. All forces must be gathered to fight the anti-Christ. "The Book of Revelation tells us that there will be numerous calamities preceding Armageddon," says a Centerite. "These revelations are being borne out every day," a female member says. This type of attitude gives the ideology of the Center an "other-worldly" nature—the dogma of the Center is not designed to overcome the existing evils in a constructive or practical manner, but to highlight the "evil and wickedness" of the contemporary society. "If we will only turn to the Bible, all will be well," said an elderly woman.

The chiliastic attitude is reflected in the timetable which

the Center believes the Communists have for taking over various countries and portions of the world.

I have verified through General Carlos Romulo, Philippine Ambassador, that the "Political Transmission No. 14" of the Philippine Islands' Communist Party, gives the timetable for the internal conquest of those 7,000 lovely islands by the end of 1961 or early 1962. India and Japan are scheduled to fall to Communism by 1965. Canada is quietly serving the Communist purpose. The encirclement is coming.[34]

The dogma of the Center is, then, composed of fundamentalistic religious ideology and political themes which espouse a conspiracy theory of history. The Center is in reaction against the dominant society because of this combination of ideologies. The point to be made is that by adopting a restrictive type of religious ideology the Center automatically limited its appeal. An organization like the Birch Society, though, utilizes a religious ideology which is not really designed to attract people but certainly is designed not to offend anybody. The Birch Society has confined itself to political protest, while the Center has included a religious protest. This means, then, that the Center could be called more "sectarian" than the Birch Society.

A question that can legitimately be asked at this point is: "Why does a person like Billy James Hargis, who describes himself as a 'fundamentalist and proud of it,' have a larger following than Huss?" He, too, sees the battle against communism as a moral battle. The several basic reasons why Hargis has a large organization all indicate that our four variables—recruitment, leadership, themes, and religion—must be viewed in relationship to each other within the particular movement. One of them is the population that the Center draws on as opposed to the one Hargis, or another national rightist leader, draws on. The Center's program is a "local" one in the sense that it generally deals with problems relating to Oregon. Hargis's organization, operating out of Tulsa, Oklahoma, attacks the "communist menace" in all states, and deals with international communism. It is interesting to note that when I questioned Huss about the success of Hargis's organization he said, "Yes, people give him a lot of money. He [Hargis] tells everyone that he is solving all of these problems, but he isn't. He has such a broad program. . . . It's not very definite." Whereas Oregon has one of the lowest nationwide percentages of church attenders, Oklahoma has one of the highest. The factor of low church attendance in Oregon may contribute to the apparent narrowness of Huss's potential source of support.[35]

Purely in terms of geographic locations, Hargis's fundamentalist orientation has a greater chance of succeeding. These factors must be viewed in combination with other elements such as personality, themes, and recruitment. Hargis has delegated authority and has paid office staff as well as a staff that accompanies him in the field. He delegates authority in an effective manner. As Huss himself noted, Hargis's themes are wide ranging. His public appearances are designed to cause excitement and win new recruits.

The program of the Birch Society, as outlined by Robert Welch, makes use of the themes of a more moderate religion. The use that is made of religion tends to integrate the organization with the social structure rather than to alienate it. There is a difference between saying, as Huss has, that: "The Devil is coming to destroy America. . . . Communism is an enemy of Jesus Christ. . . . The Center (is) . . . an arm of the Body of Christ" and saying, as Welch has, that: "Communists work for the gradual but complete destruction of the three great human loyalties—to God, to family and to country.[36]

The society is composed of "Men and women of integrity and purpose building rededication to God, to family, to country, and to strong moral principles," says Welch.[37] The purpose of religion outlined in *The Blue Book* is to give man "faith." It is this faith which will underlie the new morality which will be necessary for defeating communism.[38] It is the same type of religion that formed the basis for Moral Rearmament. It talks about man's relationship to God in metaphysical terms not used by most fundamentalists. This is a more sophisticated approach which sees religion as creating unity and harmony so that the battle can be won. Within this larger "theological setting" many beliefs can be accommodated. A person with fundamentalistic religious learnings may be attracted to the John Birch Society because of its conservative economic doctrine, and still see the battle as one of the Devil against Christ. An "unchurched" businessman will come to the movement because of its stand on economic policies, but will not be concerned with the religious aspects of the conflict. Broyles found the latter situation prevailing in the society.

Many among the Birch Society leaders and regular members I interviewed had no active religious affiliation—and none had more than nominal affiliation.[39]

Our proposition, then, is that the use made of religion by the Center is "sect-like," while the John Birch Society makes use of a "church-like" religion. In order to develop this idea we must be more specific when we speak of sects.

THE SECT MOVEMENT

The Freedom Center represents in many respects a new type of organization—one that combines religion and politics in an aggressive attack on the social world. The appearance of this type of formal organization points to a need to reexamine some of the classical terminology relating to sects and social movements. In the past, although a politically oriented group might employ certain types of religious symbolism, this did not make it a religious group. The counterpart of this situation, a religious group of adherents actively advocating some type of political action, has not really existed in this country. Religion has traditionally formed the rearguard of conservatism and has only played a post-hoc role in supporting social action. However, a changing society gives birth to many new forms. Some will be nurtured for a short while and then die, while others seem to recur under favorable circumstances.

William Jennings Bryan and Huey Long were two of the first national leaders to combine religious and political ideology in the same program. Bryan's appeal for the free coinage of silver was an appeal to fundamentalistic politico-religious values. Long's "Wealth for the Millions" platform, again, appealed to a combination of religious and political values. Examples like this are still part of the American scene, which is not surprising if we consider the theses of Will Herberg[40] and Peter Berger.[41] Herberg, in *Protestant, Catholic, Jew,* points out that the American way of life is in many respects a religious way of life. Berger, when talking about the "religious establishment" in this country, says that ". . . the churches operate with secular values while the secular institutions are permeated with religious terminology."[42] It is worth noting, then, what the component elements of these ambivalent organizations are.

THE PROBLEM

A serious drawback to many typologies is that they allow only limited inclusion of relevant conceptual material. A problem arises when these models do not permit the classification of data in expansion and modification of the original scheme.

We may keep this in mind while dealing with the concept of "sect" as defined and expanded by Weber and Troeltsch. The former saw the sect as a Christian group which rigorously enforces behavior requirements and rejects its cultural milieu.[43] Troeltsch's definition of the sect is composed of similar variables: sects are small groups which aspire to inward perfection and aim at a direct personal friendship within the group.[44] A problem arises with the polar concepts of church and sect that Weber and Troeltsch developed. Weber and Troeltsch (and many who have followed their lead) concentrated on the distinction between the sect and the church and failed to divorce these two concepts. The church was simply viewed as an outgrowth of the sect.

Let us refocus the study of the sect to provide a method that will allow us to categorize adequately and study a sect which is both politically and religiously oriented. The previous historical emphasis on the study of the sect has tended to polarize it to the church. Here we will deal with it in relation to several typologies.

THE SECT

For immediate purposes we will adopt a broad definition of the "sect." Russell R. Dynes sees the sect as a type of social organization which rejects integration with the social order and develops a separate subculture, stressing rather rigid behavior requirements for its members.[45] Many esoteric distinctions have arisen with the sect-category itself. For example, E. T. Clark distinguishes seven types.[46]

The Freedom Center's membership is characterized by three essential phenomena: 1) it is old; 2) it is essentially lower class; and 3) it is fundamentalistic. The dogma of the Center is an aggressive attack on the structure of several basic social institutions. It could be argued, then, that the Center is a sect because of its distinctive social structure, and its rejection of contemporary society. The strong religious overtones in the Center's publications and their meetings raise a related question. Is this a religious movement?

IS THE MOVEMENT A RELIGION?

The question can legitimately be raised as to whether or not the movement is a religion. In determining what leads to states of social solidarity, Émile Durkheim focused on the ensemble of beliefs and sentiments that were common to the average members of a particular society. These beliefs and sentiments were thought to form a system which had a life of its own and which represented the collective consciousness. At a minimum the characteristics of a religion are beliefs and rites. A religious rite is to be distinguished from its secular counterpart by the nature of the object concerned. For example, a law as well as a rite may prescribe some behavior; but the religious prescription refers to a different class of objects. The religious object is sacred and the secular object profane, though what is sacred varies with the society. However, the "circle of sacred objects," although it cannot be rationally defined, is actually the collective consciousness. Therefore, wherever a body of men shares a feeling that a specific group of objects is sacred and has elaborated this feeling into a specific set of beliefs and rituals, it can be said that religion exists. We have pointed out already a few of the commonly held beliefs of Center members such as their belief in a communist conspiracy, their opposition to the civil rights movement, their opposition to the U.N., their belief that there has been a breakdown in morals, and so forth. There is, then, a common set of beliefs. And there was a high consistency of attitudes, as we saw, among the members.

There is a distinctive ritual system with accepted symbols whose meaning is shared by Center members. The Pledge of Allegiance, the singing of the national anthem, and the invocation at each meeting are part of the ritual. If any one of them were omitted, people would feel uneasy. The presence of the American flag is felt to be so reassuring that it is used on cars or house windows, and flown from antennas and flagpoles whenever any occasion warrants it. Certain conservative literature is treated as if it represented a sacred text. The Center member is part of a distinctive group, and his sense of self-importance is enhanced by his various symbols of participation in it. Members visit among themselves, support one another's self-images and views of the world. There is a turning-in among the members that might be regarded as cult-like.

Yinger, realizing that the distinctions drawn by Troeltsch would not allow one either to explain adequately the development of or to categorize upper-class sects such as Christian Science or the Oxford Group Movement, expanded Troeltsch's typology. Using two criteria—the degree of inclusiveness of the members of a society and the degree of attention to the function of social integration as contrasted with the function of personal need—he developed a six-step classification which is as follows:

1. The Universal Church
2. The Ecclesia
3. The Class Church or Denomination
4. The Established Sect
5. The Sect
6. The Cult[47]

In his discussion of the cult, Yinger states that: "Pure type cults are not common in Western Society; most groups that might be called cults are fairly close to the 'sect' type. Perhaps the best examples are the various Spiritualist groups and some of the 'Moslem' groups among American Negroes."[48] Cults are essentially retreatist in nature. The Freedom Center, although it rejects the dominant society, is not retreatist. There is an active attempt to change the society through political action. A cult is, however, a group whose existence depends on a charismatic leader. One could argue that because Huss is not a charismatic leader, the group is not a cult. However, this does not appear to be a valid criticism of why the movement is or is not a cult. Max Weber sheds light on this problem when he refers to a *charismatic situation.*[49] Although the *charismatic* leader may no longer be present, the movement will still tend to be shaped by his initial influence in conjunction with certain secular factors. If Huss were to die, however, the Center would break up unless his wife, or someone equally committed, were to assume control, although as we noted earlier, people are attracted to the Center in spite of Huss. The cult is also characterized by its small size. The Center is not small. It is reasonable to conclude that the Center is not a cult. Is it an "established sect?"

Again employing Yinger's terminology, the Center is in the transition from "sect" to "established sect," embodying characteristics of both. It is an established sect because it has "professional" leaders; for example, there have at times been paid editors and speakers, and Huss, of course, draws his income from the group. Although Yinger does not include this in his scheme, evidences of material wealth would seem to be a good indication that a group has become "bureaucratized."

Another important point is that in an established sect their direct opposition to certain facets of the established social order has subsided in their drive for "respectability." If a group wants to increase its social base, it must stop attacking the base from which it will draw its support. Huss's attacks on those who disagree with him were not designed to win a broad base of support. To some extent, he made suspect any legitimate opposition to communism. The movement tends to be a sect because of its political stand, the stress on group unity, and the rigid ideological requirements expected of adherents.

One could argue that the Center was either a sect, or an established sect. *Where does this leave us?* We find that the definitions laid down by Troeltsch do not allow us to categorize adequately this movement, nor does the extension of his typology by Yinger. It is possible to view this movement in a dynamic state of transition from the sect to the established sect. However, some groups never go beyond this point. Yinger in his discussion of the sect points to some characteristics of groups at this stage. He says that when there is an undesirable situation to which a group is reacting three things can be done—the group may accept it, avoid it, or seek ways to aggressively oppose it. He then makes the point that all three of these responses may be found in what he calls a *"sect movement"*[50] although one will usually predominate. We will here define a sect movement as:

1. A group that has been formed because of some definite social need felt by the adherents.
2. A group that stands in opposition to some segment of the established social order.
3. A group that is both religiously and politically oriented.
4. A group which has specified doctrines, beliefs, and behavioral requirements.
5. A group that tends toward permanency in its institutional structure.

By the elements employed in this definition, the Freedom Center is a sect movement. The question of the differences between a sect movement and a social movement now presents itself.

THE SECT AS A SOCIAL MOVEMENT

J. Stewart Burgess has defined a social movement as a "joint endeavor of a considerable group of persons to alter or change the course of events by their activities."[51] Theodore Able extends this when he says that "collective effort may be called a social movement only if it operates with the medium of a community."[52] Thus we see that two criteria for a social movement are that it be a large effort and that there be a concerted attempt to change certain elements of the prevailing social system by generally accepted means. It would be difficult to argue that the Center is a social movement. Their active supporters are few and the ideology and means of the Center are rejected by the middle class.

The Center does, however, fit the criteria of a sect movement. First, the group was formed by Walter Huss because he and others were worried about the "insidious communist menace threatening our country." It may be inferred that the social need felt by the adherents was a concern for their own welfare as well as that of the country. Second, the group stands in opposition to several segments of the established social order. For instance, they oppose the collection of the federal income tax and believe the federal government should sell all of its "businesses," as well as stop the flow of money from this country in the form of foreign aid. Third, the group has a dual religious and political orientation. The adherents of the movement have God on their side and with His help will "lick" the Communists. Also, the meetings are characterized by definite religious overtones. Fourth, the group tends toward permanency in its institutional structure by virtue of the ownership of at least some property. The fifth category offers some difficulties. The Freedom Center has no actual specified doctrine of beliefs and behavioral requirements other than their avowal of being Christian and anti-communist. However, there is a complex pattern of behavioral syndromes which center around anti-communism and Christianity, and thus it can be said that the group does actually have a rigid doctrine, although not institutionalized. This is partly evidenced by the numerous themes which we have seen to be present in the Center's publications. In Yinger's terms, aggressiveness—in the case of the Freedom Center, aggressiveness directed against "godless communism"—predominates over the responses of avoidance or acceptance.[53]

It appears, then, that the Center, being both religiously and politically oriented, fits our ideal *"sect movement"* category.

CONCLUSION

The Freedom Center, then, is a group which is both politically and religiously oriented. It makes use of a fundamentalistic type religion and this is one of the reasons why it will most likely remain a sect. On the other hand, the Birch Society has not combined religious protest with political protest and therefore maintains a broader base in society than does the Center. As we saw, there were other phenomena which tended to limit any future growth of the Center.

WHAT IS THE FREEDOM CENTER?

In terms of the typology we examined we must view the Center as more sectarian than the Birch Society. The society possesses some of the characteristics of the church—it is large and relatively non-revolutionary—but it, too, falls toward the sect end of the church-sect continuum. The typology of the sect-movement is useful for studying the small group which has a political and religious orientation. With it, one can more adequately understand the inherent factors that limit the growth and development of an organization like the Freedom Center.

5

FINANCIAL SOURCES

One of the primary concerns of Walter and Rosalie Huss and their board of directors is where to get enough money to continue their operations. Not one publication goes out that does not include some appeal for funds. The Center's efforts at expansion and its activities are determined almost solely by the amount of money they have. The methods employed by Billy James Hargis, Carl McIntire, and other national rightist leaders are different from those employed by Walter Huss. At a public meeting of Hargis's you find him exhorting the audience as McIntire would:

Lord, who'll help fight the devil Communism? . . . Who'll give a thousand dollars. Lord, who'll give a thousand. There's a hand . . . I see a hand . . . God Bless you sir. Stand up, tell the audience your name. . . . Are there any more fine people in the audience this evening? Yes, yes, there's another. Anymore, anymore . . . who'll give five hundred. . . .[1]

And Hargis continues until he is asking for twenty-dollar donations. It is not uncommon for him, or a person like Carl McIntire, to raise two to three thousand dollars from a large audience in less than fifteen minutes. When Huss asks the public for funds at a gathering, the method, as well as the amount of money collected, is different. In a public meeting,

Huss usually says that money is needed to carry on the fight. A prayer is said and envelopes or a paper bucket are passed down the aisle. Nothing more is said.

How has the Center been financed?

THE EAGLE

Since the beginning of 1962 the Center has published the *National Eagle*. It has subscribers and solicits advertising. Is this a source of funds? When the paper was first published, a year's subscription cost $5.00, and one could have a three-month trial subscription for $1.00. Individual papers cost ten cents. During 1962 eleven editions of the paper were published, which meant that if you had subscribed for a year the paper cost you almost fifty cents a copy. In 1963 the subscription rate was still $5.00 a year, but apparently only five editions of the *Eagle* were published. This meant that people were paying $1.00 a copy. In 1964 the rate was still the same and eight copies were published. During this time, the *Eagle* continued to tell subscribers that if enough contributions were given, the *Eagle* would "fly weekly" at no additional cost to subscribers. The subscription rate was a means of subsidizing some Center activities as well as the paper's publication. It does not cost $1.00 to publish and distribute an eight-page tabloid.

In 1965 the Center began the publication of a regional *Eagle*, with offices in Medford, Oregon. Subscriptions, for a paper that was supposed to be a weekly, were $1.00 for one month or $3.00 for a year's subscription or $5.00 by mail. As noted in the *Eagle*, however, it would have cost $67.50 per 1,000 papers to produce and deliver them. The paper would have cost well over the six cents per issue a regular subscriber would pay, and the Center would not make any money on their paper. In addition, a letter from Walter Huss dated December 8, 1964, said that the *Eagle* would begin by being mailed to every home in Jackson County, which is in Southern

Oregon, each week for four weeks, under the assumption that subscribers would be brought in. To do this subsidization would be necessary. An advertisement in the *Eagle,* as well as personal letters, asked members and others to help. The money was not available to send free copies to all homes in the county. Instead, workers in the area called people whose names were listed in the phone book and asked them if they would like to receive a free copy of the *Eagle.* From my observations of a mailing list compiled at the Portland center, it appeared that only two or three hundred people had been selected by this method to receive free copies.

The situation, then, appears to be this. The *Eagle* merged with the *Northwest Sentinel* in 1962, and thus it had for some time, at least, a ready-made list of subscribers from whom to receive funds. When the paper was being sold at a subscription rate of $5.00 per year, and less than twelve issues were published a year, the Center made money. This assumes, of course, that they were not publishing free copies. However, one of their apparent techniques for drawing people in is to put them on their mailing list, and send them several free copies of their publications in the hope that they will become supporters. This practice tends to use up extra funds. Further, an examination of cost per paper of publication, compared to the cost of a year's subscription, indicates that the Center is losing money. Of course a paper rarely makes costs from its subscription rates. Papers make money through advertising.

Is advertising a source of revenue for the Center?

ADVERTISING

The percentage of advertising space in the *Eagle* is extremely small. In 1962 eight of eleven issues had absolutely no advertising. The only ads which appeared were those of the Center, telling people that certain films and tapes could be rented. Finally a few ads appeared which were placed by private parties and small businesses.

Several other things can be noted about the *Eagle* ads. First, not all of those are probable sources of revenue. Several of the ads for Sunrise Fuel Co. stated that Sunrise would support the *Eagle* financially if people would buy oil from them. "For every gallon of comfort oil you buy from us, we will financially support the Freedom Center Educational Program!"[2] It is unlikely that Sunrise paid for this ad.

Another advertisement, one for Berg's St. Johns Funeral Home, did not appear until April 1963. On February 20, 1963, the Huss' child, Theodore Mark Huss, the youngest of seven children, died. Funeral services were arranged by St. Johns Funeral Home. It is unlikely that the Bergs would have advertised in the *Eagle* because they thought it a "good" place to solicit business. Similar personal contacts appear to have operated in the case of other ads. Small ads which bring in little revenue have been placed by Center members who own their own businesses.

A study of the number of ads, then, indicates that the Center's activities could not be financed through advertising. The self-sustaining paper has over 30 per cent of its total column inches devoted to advertising. The highest figure the Center ever attained was 6 per cent, and this only because the John Birch Society had a full-page ad—the only full-page ad that ever appeared in the *Eagle.* If we discount the ad placed by the society, the 1964 percentage total is even smaller than in 1963, slightly less than 4 per cent. Advertising is not a source of funds for the Center.

JOB PRINTING

In the basement of the Freedom Center in Portland, Oregon, is sufficient equipment to make the Center one of the larger job printing businesses in the city. As an ad of theirs which runs frequently in the *Eagle* notes, they are equipped to make plates and print bulletins, brochures, letters, forms, letterheads, handbills, do composing work, make up layouts, and make negatives and halftones. They will also make address plates and do mailing for any firm or club. They have not, as a former editor of their paper stated, tried to develop this potential. They run their ad, but do relatively little soliciting for job printing. Occasionally they print brochures, business cards, church programs, and booklets for business firms. There is a small amount of income derived, then, from job printing. But the potential has not been utilized.

FILMS, TAPES, AND PUBLICATIONS

The amount of money received during the last six months of 1960 for equipment, tapes, and films was $2,534.75. During 1961 and 1962 the Center listed films available under two plans. You could either pay a minimum $15.00 rental fee, or you could have a Freedom Center representative show the film and take a free will offering. There were also two film strips available for $5.00. Until early 1964, most of these films were in demand. People reported in 1965 that they had seen several of these films more than once. A former editor of the *Eagle* was asked if many of the films were rented. He indicated that as far as he knew none of them were being requested. This represented the situation, then, in early 1965.

The same situation prevails with the many tapes available from the Center. Recordings were made of all the programs the Center sponsored and most of these were available on request. Originally the sale of tapes ran behind the rental of films; in 1965 the sale of tapes by the Center was almost nonexistent, even though a 1962 publication listed fifty-one of them as being available.

A major source of revenue for the Center appears to have come from their long list of available publications, reprints, and articles. The works of Dr. Fred Schwarz, Herbert Philbrick, J. Edgar Hoover, Barry Goldwater, C. W. Burpo, Carl McIntire, and many others are available from the Center. Small booklets which cost from five cents to fifteen cents each, with titles like "Christ Is Answer to Red Threat," and "Shall We Allow The Family To Be Destroyed?" are for sale. In some cases permission to reproduce these pamphlets has been granted to the Center; in others it has not. The Center reproduces and circulates for sale newsletters put out by various congressmen. This is usually done without permission. Material from other papers is reproduced in toto and sold. An article from *Sports Illustrated*, "Blueprint for Peace—A Threat to Gun Ownership?" was sold for ten cents during the Goldwater-Miller campaign.

The financial statement for the last six months of 1960 indicates that a total of $1,367.83 was received from the sale of literature. This is one source of revenue that has not dried up. It is, of course, not as great as it was during the presidential campaign of 1964, when many people stopped at the Center and gathered up large quantities of *all* available literature. During the campaign, people picked up one or two different paperbacks, tracts on various problems, bumper stickers, stickers for envelopes, and other paraphernalia without apparent concern for what they were buying. In some cases it represented a gesture toward helping in the campaign. It was noteworthy that during the in-depth interview conducted after Goldwater's defeat these people wanted to give away as much of the literature they had accumulated as possible.

FREEDOM SCHOOLS, SEMINARS, AND RALLIES

One of the Center's early approaches to fighting communism was to sponsor and schedule a "School of Americanism and Anti-Communism." Advertisements were run which told of rallies to last from three to six days and nights. It was also possible to have a one-day or one-night rally in a given community. Speeches would be given, tapes played, movies shown, books and pamphlets brought to make "an event long remembered." Admission was charged and books were sold. This was a source of income.

The Center also developed a "Group Plan" involving tapes and pamphlets to aid those who wished to study the problem. One plan consisted of eight separate lessons with instructions. All materials for the lessons were supplied by the Center. This type of program is similar to those used by other rightists. Carl McIntire, the home office of the John Birch Society, and the Christian Crusade under the leadership of the Reverend Billy James Hargis also have study groups. Meetings of local chapters are taken up with the reading of prepared speeches from the home office, playing prepared tapes, and studying prepared materials. These activities represent an important source of revenue for all rightist groups.

Besides the smaller group seminars and community rallies that the Center sponsored in 1961 and 1962, there were larger meetings in Portland. These meetings featured national figures like Schwarz, Skousen, Prussion, and Philbrick. A fee was charged for attending these meetings.

All of this was naturally non-profit, according to the Center. But national figures, no matter how worthy their cause, do not come free. Buildings must be rented, programs printed, phone calls have to be made. Toward the end of 1962 and early in 1963, attendance at programs began to drop off rapidly. However, when Huss conducted his rallies in small communities, free will offerings were taken and these represented a small source of income.

The Center has also held activities which cannot be called schools or rallies but can best be termed general programs. They usually feature a speaker talking on a nonpolitical topic. One example would be the program sponsored at the Freedom Center Auditorium during August, 1962. Dr. Mark Fakkema was the instructor for a Moral Training Course. Tickets were sent out and a "donation" of $10.00 was required before one could attend. Students and ministers could, however, come for half price. Any time a program like this was held an "offering" was taken in addition to the admission price. However, public meetings are not a very reliable source of revenue for the Center.

CONTRIBUTIONS AND CONTRIBUTORS

It appears that *the* main source of the Center's stable support are the frequent statements of need which the Center sends out in letter and pamphlet form. There have been various plans devised to get donations for the Center's work.

In 1961 one could become a member of Freedom Crusade if he contributed $2.00 or more per month to the cause. As was indicated, "Membership is sustained by supporting the basis and objectives of the Crusade." This program was, nevertheless, altered in 1962, and people could "Become a Charter Member of the Freedom Center's Freedom Corps," for a small amount. The fee was only a contribution of $1.00 or more each month and there were both men's and women's corps. The requirements for membership were stated as follows:

1. That you now become an active member of the Freedom Center, by pledging at least $1.00 or more per month in its support.
2. That you pledge your time and talent to some phase of the Center activity that best suits your capabilities or the daily interests that you now have.
3. That you pledge to uphold at all times the 3 purposes of Freedom Center which are:
   *To defeat the advance of communism
   *To revive the struggle for Freedom
   *To extend Freedom to all mankind[3]

This was one source of funds.

Other ads asked people to become "An American Eagle Booster." When the *Eagle* began its campaign in the southern part of the state, Huss sought contributors for several purposes. First, as was noted, he wanted people to subsidize the printing and distribution of 1,000 papers at a cost of $67.50.

Second, he wanted contributions to help support the local *Eagle* office. Finally, he wanted people to purchase gift subscriptions.

If people give, they seem to do so sporadically. In an election year, or with a special program before the community, they will give money. As Huss indicated, though, in conversations and letters, the problem was to get people to give consistently. After the Goldwater-Miller campaign, financial support dropped. Huss then instituted a new program.

In December 1964, a Christmas letter was sent from the Center which described in detail something new—"Freedom Shares." The letter pointed out that they must "consolidate" the gains made during the election and put their program on a "sustaining basis." A share would cost no more than "the price of a cup of coffee (just 10 cents) a day."

What was a Freedom Share?

A freedom share is an investment to provide increased organizational facilities and personnel to advance the program for the preservation of American freedom. This share is *a personal contribution* for as long as the support of freedom requires it.[4]

But people did not buy Freedom Shares. A former representative of the Center, Mr. James Bisel, said that even though the Husses were very excited about this program it had not been very widely received. People gave the same amounts of money that they had previously given.

Where else does money come from to finance operations? In 1964 Huss campaigned for the Republican nomination. A committee was formed and some funds were supplied. A total of $1,521.50 was raised for the campaign. There were twenty-five contributors, most of whom gave about $10.00. Some of these people gave contributions to the Center for its "educational" activities. Huss pointed out that practically all of the money for operations comes from people within the state of Oregon.

How much do they give? During the initial interviewing, and casual conversations, the members were asked this question, and the impression was that the Freedom Center is *not* financed by a wealthy few. The contributions which come in the mails are small. The amounts that people give at free will offerings are small. The Center is financed by numerous people who send in a few dollars at sporadic intervals. The audit statement for the last six months of 1960 indicated that the Center was operating with a budget slightly over $3,500 a month. Activities increased during 1961 and 1962, operating expenses went up, and so did the deficit of the Center.

The financial situation of the Center can best be described by referring to incidents. When the editor of the paper quit in March 1965, the Center was behind in his salary. Mr. Bisel was not able to sell enough "Shares for Freedom" to make this his occupation.

The Center was badly in need of repairs, and these had to be delayed. The ceiling literally dripped during rainstorms. Machines broke down and temporary repairs had to be made. When Mrs. Huss went to the post office to do mailings she had to calculate very carefully what the cost was going to be so that she could deposit enough money in their account at the post office to cover it. It was not financially possible for her to have a large post office deposit. The Huss family got by with a minimum of luxury items. Papers were stacked in corners for lack of filing cabinets. Long distance phone calls were cut to a minimum so that the phone bill did not go up. The situation was tight.

As I have indicated, during the latter part of 1963, there was a sharp drop in attendance at Center meetings. Urgent appeals were made for additional funds. But during 1964, several events at the University of Oregon as well as the presidential campaign conspired to bring the Center back into the minds of the public. After the campaign, activities again began to decline. Fewer people showed up at the Freedom Center to work or to purchase literature. There is an obvious rise and fall, then, in the Center's fortunes as local and national issues affect the number of people contributing to the Center and its programs.

Part Two
THE PEOPLE

6

BIRCHERS AND CENTERITES: ACCOUNTING FOR RADICAL RIGHTISM

THE JOHN BIRCH SOCIETY

There is a wealth of literature dealing with the problem involved in delimiting the social areas of a city,[1] and attributing certain behavior patterns found in those areas to their particular social conditions. Anyone who has attempted to characterize an entire city in terms of "areas" has one basic assumption: that people who live close together tend to be more alike than people who live far apart. The book by Shaw and McKay, *Juvenile Delinquency in Urban Areas,* postulated that delinquents will be found in certain areas of any city.[2] Homogeneity is the key to this study, as it is to any study that makes use of social areas. One problem, however, is that often aggregate data are used to make predictions about individual behavior.[3] Consequently, if one is going to try to deal with rightist behavior by constructing indices to account for it, these indices must be based on individual and not aggregate correlations.

The first problem to be dealt with is this. Given the names and addresses of 1,600 members of the John Birch Society throughout the United States, can we account for where they live in terms of indices of disorganization? (This group of 1,600 will hereafter be referred to as the McNall sample.) Do the general social areas in which these people live share a common characteristic?

In the 1964 *Bulletin* for November, Robert Welch told the followers of the John Birch Society:

On Sunday, December 6, the magnificent new Music Center will be opened in Los Angeles. Built on municipally owned land, in the Civic Center at Grand Avenue and First Street, this new pride of a great city was built with private funds, raised largely under the leadership of Mrs. Norman Chandler, who had been chairman of the building fund since the project was started in 1959. Mrs. Chandler and all of her associates are to be congratulated, and deserve great credit and much applause.

But a horrible red fly has now crawled into the ointment. At a luncheon meeting of dignitaries in the Los Angeles County Hall of Administration . . . Mr. Robert A. Riddell, coordinating chairman for the United Nations Week Activities, presented a United Nations flag for the Music Center. . . . And it was officially announced that this UN flag would be flown over the building.[4]

It is now beside the point that this story was not true. Members were urged to send an "immediate flood of letters" to nine of the sponsors, patrons, and officials of the Music Center. Among the nine were Mrs. Norman Chandler and Walt Disney, who was chairman of the Bucks Bag Committee. It is important for the representativeness of our sample that Welch's story was not carried in any other rightist publication at the time. This means that of the letters received by the nine people to whom the Birchers were supposed to write there were likely to be few from any other group.

The nine people listed in the *Bulletin* were contacted and asked if they would be willing to release the letters that they had received so that a content analysis could be made. Several of them agreed and over 1,600 letters were received for analysis. The letter-writers tended to concentrate on names that were familiar to them; thus Walt Disney received an overwhelming majority—80 per cent. A content analysis of the letters was made and one finding is of special importance here.

In the *Bulletin* for November members were told:

As always, keep your letters friendly, polite, factual, and carefully reasoned. Your most effective argument, it seems to me, might be along this line. The Music Center is a tremendous accomplishment, a tribute to the free-enterprise American system which produced the private wealth that made it possible, a tribute to the public-spiritedness of the very people to whom you are writing, and a tribute to the cultural standards of the people of Los Angeles County. It is something of which all the millions of good citizens of southern California should, and normally would, be very proud indeed. Then why on earth mar that accomplishment, dampen that enthusiasm, and needlessly convert it into a symbol of what so many millions of even these same good people in southern California, regard as a dangerous enemy of our country and threat to the future freedom of our children? . . .[5]

The *Bulletin* then went on to list the sources from which the writers could quote. In the content analysis of the 1,600 usable letters one of the things looked for was whether or not the content of the letters was the same as that suggested by the Birch Society publication. The assumption was that if it were the same, then the sample of letter-writers represented Birch Society members and not other groups. Of the total, 27 per cent of the letters took exact quotations from the *Bulletin,* 56 per cent paraphrased them, and the remaining 17 per cent did not follow the format suggested by the society. Following is an example of a paraphrased letter from a husband and wife which begins:

You are to be congratulated on your new Music Center. It is a tremendous accomplishment and a tribute to your public spiritedness and to the cultural standards of the people of Los Angeles.

It is something of which all the good citizens of Southern California should and normally would be very proud indeed. But the flying of the U.N. flag over the Music Center would only serve to mar that accomplishment, dampen that enthusiasm, and needlessly convert it into a symbol of what so many millions of even these same good people of southern California regard as a dangerous enemy of our country and a threat to the future of our children. . . .

Further confirmation that this sample is representative of the residential distribution of Bircher letter-writers comes from a comparison of two other studies of letters written by superpatriots. The first was a study conducted by Wartenburg and Thielens of a letter-writing campaign by Birchers against the United Nations.[6] The second was a study conducted by McEvoy of letters written to a national magazine protesting a story which to some rightists seemed "subversive."[7] (Here again, the monthly *Bulletin* interpreted the story as being subversive, and urged a letter-writing campaign.) A comparison of the three studies reveals marked similarities in regional distribution. (See Appendix, Table A.1.) There is a small percentage difference between the samples in terms of the representation from the South and Northeast. McNall's sample has a smaller percentage from the southern states and a greater number from the northeastern states than the earlier studies. California is separated for analysis as it accounts for one-third of all letter-writers in the three samples.

It might have been expected that the McNall sample would have had a preponderance of writers from California, as the issue of the U.N. flag over the Music Center was a local one. However, the very fact that there were no more responses from California for this cause than there had been in the other two cases indicates that McNall's sample is representative of the letter-writers and that one third of the Birch Society's members are in California. Given the fact that we have what can reasonably be called a representative sample of writers, let us see how we can account for the existence of this group of people.

As we noted previously, ideologies and area of residence

are often linked. We do know that crime rates are higher in areas of the city marked by low socioeconomic status, high in- and out-migration, and other variables characteristic of an unstable environment. We know also that in periods of general societal disorder—for example, wars or depressions—there tends to be an increase in membership in religious organizations and social movements. The general thesis that both Kornhauser and Nisbet have put forth when speaking about the mass society is that the movements or organizations which people join are a means of handling the disorganization in their environment. In the mass society those old settings in which the individual has received support for his ego—that is, his ideologies and self concepts—are fragmented. The intermediate groups which spring up in the mass society are a direct response to the social needs of the isolated person.

We know that the Birch Society has a distinctive ideology and that it represents a distinctive subculture within the larger society. Is there anything in the larger environment which can account for a person's movement into society? Note that we are not talking about what causes an individual to join the Birch Society instead of some other group. We are asking: "Are there general predisposing conditions for group membership in the larger society?" Can one derive empirical measures of a mass society?

Four indicators were taken as possible measures of dis-organization.[8] They were: 1) percentage of migration in and out of a state; 2) the number of suicides in a state; 3) the median age of the population in a state; and 4) the amount of theft and larceny in a state. We started on the state level to see whether it would be possible to account for the variation from state to state in the number of Birchers. The census data for individuals was taken for each state and inter-item correlations computed. (See Table A.2 in the Appendix for the relationship between these variables and the residential location of our group of 1600 Birchers.)

It was decided to use migration as a measure of disorganization because a high degree of migration in either direction

can cause a breakdown of stable referents. Community facilities can be strained by an influx of newcomers; strangers with
new social and physical needs can cause disruption. As for
out-migration, this could be caused by unemployment and
other factors which also signal potential disorganization. As the
figures on migration indicate, there is a strong relationship
(.51) between amount of migration and membership in the
Birch Society. This finding gives support to the notion that
rapid changes in familiar environments can act as an impetus
to radical political behavior. In the case of California, which
is second only to Nevada in amount of migration during this
period, we find a particularly strong relationship between in-
migration and membership in the Birch Society. It should
also be noted that it is in-migration and not out-migration that
seems to be related to membership in the Birch Society.

In the case of in-migration we have a situation in which
newcomers to an area may not be readily absorbed by the existing institutions and may, in fact, challenge those institutions. The newcomer to an area may feel isolated and rejected
because of different values. He may, for instance, be a recent
migrant from a stable rural area. Or he may be an old member of the community who does not accept strangers and reacts by seeking out others who share his political philosophy,
which advocates exclusion and isolation, and which sees the
newcomer as subversive. We do not know however, whether
these Birch Society members are recent migrants to the area
in which they now reside. In the case of Southern California,
where almost a third of them are located, we do know that it
is in-migration which has accounted for the society's rapid
population growth which is not due to an abnormally high
birth rate. It is likely that those who are members of the Birch
Society are also recent migrants to the area, and the in-migrat-
ing population is likely to contribute a greater share to the
Society than does the general population.

The number of suicides is a classic measure of the amount
of disorganization in a given area. As Émile Durkheim pointed
out, anomic suicide was a direct response to a situation in

which the individual could no longer orient himself to a familiar world.[9] Old norms, rules, and definitions of situations being no longer adequate, the individual was disoriented and usually isolated from the protective influences of a primary group. His alternatives were to reintegrate with a social body or to commit suicide. But in a state of maximum disorganization, the individual's opportunities to integrate into an ongoing social group and to protect his ego are limited.

The data analysis indicates that the relationship between migration and suicide is substantial (.52). However, there is a lower-order relationship between suicide and rightist behavior (.27). This raises the question of alternatives. We can speculate that in an area characterized by disorganization (as measured by migration), there is a tendency for deviant behavior to occur. This is why there is a strong relationship between migration and suicide and migration and rightist behavior, but not between suicide and rightist behavior. Both are responses to disorganization. But to the extent that suicide is another alternative to rightist membership, we would expect a high negative correlation between suicide and rightism, both on an individual and a state basis. This is partly true, but we have other variables operating. Suicides do occur in places in which there are high rates of disorganization. So does rightist behavior. Consequently, we have this relationship between suicide and rightist behavior. This means that suicide and rightism are two ways of handling the same problem. If one alternative is taken (and the most frequently chosen is group membership), then the other alternative will not be. But to underline the fact, *disorganization* (and suicide is a direct reflection of disorganization) *is related to rightism.*

That suicide is a variable of a different level is evidenced by an examination of two other measures of disorganization. As can be seen from Table A.2 in the Appendix, theft relates to rightism (.38) as does larceny (.48). A much higher relationship exists, however, between these variables and migration (both at the .67 level). The relationship between suicide and theft is .35 and between suicide and larceny it is .50. One may interpret all of these relations as follows.

In these cases, migration is the independent variable, and larceny, theft, suicide, and rightism are responses to it—but on different levels. The mobility of people into and out of a region generates anomie for several reasons. As noted above, when the movement is outward, it may signal the dissolution of old ties and the breakup of friendship patterns which contribute to individual stability. Where the movement is inward, it can strain established relationships and organizations that are not equipped to assimilate the newcomers. There are two levels of response to changing definitions of the situation. One may opt out of the system by committing suicide, or one can respond to the changes.

As Kai Erickson has pointed out, deviance, which contributes to and is the result of disorganization, is one way in which a society defines its boundaries.[10] Deviance, quite simply, is what a society chooses *to label* as deviant. The function of the society's labeling is to make disorganization a means for defining the boundaries of the system. In this sense, moderate disorganization can be thought of as system-maintaining. This applies to our case, because rightism can be considered a response to the changing boundaries. It is an attempt on the part of the people involved to find themselves in the system. This search is a complicated process, and involves an attempt to find validation for a way of life and an image of it. Theft and larceny are also responses to the changes in the boundaries brought on by migration. The opportunities for deviant acts may increase as the boundaries change. However, there is a lower order of relationship between theft and larceny and rightism because of different responses to boundaries. High migration can contribute to high crime rates, and rightist political behavior often springs up in these areas. But the rightist's response is to support drives to hire more police and define the boundaries so that "criminal" behavior is brought under control. This would lower the rates of crime and consequently lower the relationship between crime and rightism, but would maintain a stronger relationship between rightism and migration because migration is the independent variable.

The one measure of disorganization which seemed to have no relationship to rightism was age. Age was included in these measures because in an urban setting the old are often cut off from those ties which are necessary to maintain a sense of integrity and general well-being. In addition, the composition of some radical right groups has often been envisioned as made up of the elderly, and the elderly tend to live in urban areas and not in the suburbs. However, this is a sample of members of the Birch Society, and Birchers tend to be fairly well-educated, financially secure, and thus likely to be living in the suburbs.

Much has been made of the relationship between rightism and fundamentalistic religion. When people think of radical rightists they often think of men like Billy James Hargis, Carl McIntire, and others who combine a fundamentalist rhetoric with their politics. In addition, attention has been given to the fact that religions in this country generally support the status quo and also call for support for values and ways of life that are characteristic of the nineteenth century. It is reasonable to conjecture that because of these relationships, religion would be related to membership in rightist groups such as the Birch Society.

Three variables were selected in order to deal with this question. The first—the per cent of total population who are Protestants—is a rough indicator of how many people in a given state profess membership in a given church. It also provides a rough estimate of how many people are likely to go to church. The next category, the percent of church-goers according to religious faith, is the number of Protestants divided by the number of members in all other religious faiths. This category was included along with the first so that we would have some idea of the number of Catholics in a given state. This way we could test assumptions relating Catholicism and increasing conservatism in some segments of the Catholic Church to conservative politics. Finally, we wished to isolate the Fundamentalists for separate analysis because they possess an eschatological ideology which is similar in content to much of the ideology of radical rightists. Also, it was necessary to isolate the Fundamentalists from the main body of Protestants because some states are dominated by liberal Protestant denominations such as the Methodists.

The first fact that is evidenced from Table A.2 is the lack of any relationship between rightism and religion. Two things are operating here—the nature of the sample and the relationship of religion with our other variables. Our measures of disorganization—for example, migration, suicide, theft, and larceny—are all negatively related to religion. This can be explained by the fact that membership in religious bodies is not related to high rates of disorganization. (One of the major problems facing the urban church is how to retain its membership.) As for the sample, it can be noted that although the bulletins of the Birch Society stress support for religious values they do not incorporate religion as part of their appeal. The only appeals are the vague "mother, God, and country" type. In addition, membership in rightist groups may partially substitute for membership in religious bodies. Primarily, Table VI.2 shows that membership in rightist groups and membership in religious bodies are independent phenomena.

The information up to this point does not furnish us with data on individual behavior, nor does it allow us to adequately answer the question "How do you account for rightist behavior?" We have, however, gone part of the way. There is a strong relationship between disorganization at the state level and rightist membership in a particular state, but we do not know whether this disorganization operates on a local level. In short, do rightists live in *areas* of a state or in *areas* of cities characterized by disorganization and, if so, is it this disorganization that accounts for their joining a rightist group?

THE CASE OF CALIFORNIA

Southern California is the undisputed center of Birch activity in the United States. One third of our sample and one third of the Michigan and Columbia samples are concentrated there. Does Southern California differ significantly from the rest of California? Let us examine the counties. Sixty-eight percent of all Birchers in our sample live in five counties. These counties comprise 53 per cent of the total population of California. We selected six variables for comparing these counties with the remainder of California's counties. The percent of increase in population from the 1950 to 1960 census was taken as a measure of disorganization. We did not use the items of theft, larceny, and so forth, as we did in our comparisons of states, because, as we have seen, these variables are highly related to amounts of migration. As some rightist propaganda has often had a distinct ethnocentric bias and because Southern California has a large proportion of foreign-born people, we included a measure of the percentage of foreign born. The populations were also compared in terms of median years of school, rates of unemployment, number of professionals in the civilian labor force, and median family income. This is due to the fact that Birchers, as Lipset indicates in his review of the data from California, tend to be fairly well educated and middle-class.[11] (See Table A.3 in the Appendix for the relevant comparisons.)

It is immediately evident when one examines the data that the major difference between these five counties and the rest of California is in the increase in population between 1950 and 1960. While the total state experienced an overall increase in population by 48.5 percent, all except one of our five counties far surpassed that figure. The county of Santa Clara, for instance, had an increase in population of 121.1 percent. There is a distinction between the other five variables for the specific counties. This distinction is not, however, consistent. What *can* be said is that the only significant variation comes in migration, which is taken as a measure of disorganization.[12] There is increasing evidence that disorganization can account for membership in rightist organizations like the Birch Society, but this proposition needs to be tested at still another level. Can rates of disorganization within a city and/or a city's census tracts account for differential rates in membership in rightist groups? To test this proposition we will make use of another sample.

THE FREEDOM CENTER

The reason for changing samples is that in some cases the home address of our Birch sample was not obtainable. For example, the person may have signed his name but neglected to include a street address. The postmark was usually used to locate him in a town, but we could not locate the town's census tracts. Also, it would be almost impossible to construct indices for social disorganization for every census tract for every city in the United States. There would be further problems in comparing different cities, regions, and so forth. Consequently, we concentrated on one city for which we had an identifiable sample of active members. As we are postulating that the same factors will contribute to participation in all radical-rightist movements it does not matter whether we shift from Birchers to Freedom Center members. This point will be raised again as it bears on the problem of "availability" of movements.

The sample of Center members was collected, as has already been noted, as a result of involvement as a participant observer in a radical-rightist organization. In the course of this study we were able to obtain the names and addresses of 266 members in Portland, Oregon. This was a complete listing of all those who had contributed money and time to the organization. It was a list of *involved* participants. Without going into detail, it should be noted that this group's membership was composed primarily of lower to lower middle-class men and women, most of them over the age of fifty, who lived in an urban area. The organization was also made up of people who had fundamentalist religious backgrounds, and the rhetoricians from this background found continual expression in the meetings of the Freedom Center.

Our problem in dealing with the location of the residences of 266 Center members was to try and account for this location in a systematic fashion. We constructed two indices—one of social status, and one of disorganization. The index of social status was made up of the following variables: average value of dwelling, average contract rent, median years of school completed, median family income, and percentage of labor force employed.[13] (See Table A.4 in the Appendix.) These variables are highly correlated, but are they "logically" related? The median income of a family, by itself, will not be a good representation of social status, but combined with such factors as the median years of school completed for the population in the census tract, it takes on more meaning. A high income, a high education, and an expensive home is an even better indicator. Yet all of this could occur in a disintegrating area, as measured by low rents and the number of unemployed. We then listed the pertinent information for each of our five variables for ninety-five census tracts. In the case of four census tracts, which comprise a major part of Portland's skid row, "arbitrary" rankings had to be given. After listing all of the necessary information for the census tracts and then ranking *each* census tract in terms of the particular values for that tract, we arbitrarily assigned the lowest ranks to skid row. Next, after having ranked each census tract for five variables with possible ranks of 1 to 96, we calculated the average rank for each census tract. Theoretically, it was possible for a census tract to have an average rank running from 1 to 96; the actual range was from 3 to 95. Finally, we ranked the average ranks so that the values ranged from 0 to 95. The reason for doing this was to facilitate the statistical comparison between this measure and the measure of social disorganization to follow. (The Spearman rank order correlation between the measure of social status and the measure of social disorganization for the selected census tracts is $-.70$.) We then divided this scale into eight parts, for the purpose of constructing a graphic scale to depict the various social status "areas" of the city. The names and addresses of the 266 Center members were then plotted and compared with the eight areas. (The results are indicated in Table A.4 of the Appendix.) An inspection of the data indicates that the percentage of members found in a given social area differs from the percentage of the total population for that area in an "inverse" manner. There is a slightly smaller percentage of members in high social status areas compared to the percentage of the population for the given area. Conversely, in the lower status social areas there is a greater percentage of members than would be expected on the basis of simply the percentage of total population for that area. It would appear, on the basis of this information, that there has been a tendency for Centerites to be concentrated in the low-status areas of the city.

However, if we use the percentage of total population for a given social area to compute the expected frequency of occurrence for residence of Center members, we find that our X^2 is not significant at the .05 level. A clear trend appears, however, even though it is not statistically significant. Perhaps the explanation is to be found by looking at areas of social disorganization.

In our measure of social disorganization we included the variables percentage of dwelling units deteriorating and dilapidated; percentage of black population; rate of family disruption; and median age of males.[14] Of course a high percentage of black people in a census tract does not mean high rates of social disorganization. The contrary may be the case where there is a closely-knit ethnic group that punishes deviations. Yet when one combines the various factors which compose our index of disorganization, the situation changes radically. The procedure here was the same as that for the last index in terms of assignment of values and ranking of the census tracts. Again the residences of the 266 Centerites were compared to the resulting areas. (Table A.5 in the Appendix gives the results of this analysis.) It was found that six of the eight percentages occur in an expected direction. The total percentage difference in the expected direction for social status, however, was approximately 20 per cent, while it is in actuality only 11.72 per cent. (The corresponding X^2 is also lower for Table A.5 than for the previous one.) In this case disorganization per se does not account for rightist behavior in this city.

In order to determine whether or not an index combining low social status with high rates of disorganization would afford a better predictive device we combined all of the indices. Following the same procedures as for the separate indices, it was found that all of the percentage differences were in the expected direction, and the results were significant at the .10 level. But the relevant point is that, again, we could not adequately account for rightist political behavior by the use of demographic data alone. Another variable operates.

In his discussion of the peyote religion among the Navaho, David F. Aberle uses a model that has relevance here. In order to account for the level of peyote use in specific areas, Aberle took into account more than a dozen variables that have been used to study Navaho culture. Towaoc was the community that had the earliest history of extensive peyote use, and it was found that the use of peyote in other Navaho communities could be best accounted for by their distance from Towaoc.

The best predictor for early peyotism is the availability measure—mileage from Towaoc, in a logarithmic transformation. The shorter the distance the higher level of peyotism. . . .[15]

The concept of availability can also account for membership in other organizations. Availability means more than how close a person is to the source of a phenomenon. It also has to do with the number of intervening opportunities which present themselves.[16] In the case of the peyote users there were, for example, few other religious organizations, fraternal organizations, and so forth. Availability therefore involves at least two major variables—distance from the phenomenon and/or the number of alternatives available to an individual for involving himself in some other group.

This applies to the Freedom Center in two ways. First, 25 percent of the members lived within the census tract of the Center, or in ones immediately adjacent. Second, and more important, the members' opportunities to become involved in this organization were rigidly channeled. As will be seen, friendship matrices account for much of the membership.

It was possible to interview a random sample of fifty-four people out of the original list of 266. In asking these people about other affiliations it was found that 72 per cent of them had been concentrated, previous to joining the Center, in four fundamentalistic churches. Even among the remaining 28 percent there was evidence that they had had old friends in the Center before they had become members, or that they had recruited friends. (Obviously there are cases where, because of a person's interest in radical groups, he will be independently attracted to the group and does not fit into a friendship matrix.) Two factors are operating in the case of this organization: distance, and the number of other organizations around. Both of these dimensions constitute availability.

AN APPLICATION

Could this analysis apply to our Birch sample? Let us extend it and consider what follows in terms of possible explanations. At this stage, we are not seeking definitive statements, but suggestive ones. The available data limit the conclusions that we can draw, but it need not limit our perspectives.

We cannot trace out the friendship matrices, but we can deal with one of the other dimensions of availability—that is, what other alternatives present themselves to a person who is predisposed to join a deviant political organization. If we assume that the mass society thesis is sound, that intermediate associations, for example, arise as a means of dealing with problems of alienation (the greater the disorganization the greater the number of intermediate associations), then we can postulate that in those areas where disorganization is high, there will be more Birch activity. We have seen that there is a strong relationship between disorganization and residential location of Birchers and Centerites. By this logic one could explain the high concentration of Birch membership in Southern California, and in California in general. It was *the* available organization for people who were predisposed by disorganization to join a movement. California experienced a rapid rate of population growth and, as we noted previously, the old associations were not capable of assimilating the newcomers. When an organization such as the Birch Society came along it served a double purpose. On the one hand, it channeled the impulses of people who were predisposed to this type of group into a singular activity and, on the other, it served as a means of assimilating a new population. In short, the Birch Society is successful in California because there was not a series of older established groups to which people with deviant impulses could be attracted. Had there been a choice of similar organizations there first, the Birch Society would not have the strength it does.

In order to support this line of reasoning further, let us turn to the South. On the basis of our indicators, we would expect that, because many areas of the South are characterized by disorganization, they would also be prime areas in which the Birch Society might grow. But the Birch Society is not dominant in the South. We contend that this is because people who would be likely to join the Society have been channeled into organizations such as the White Citizens Councils and the Ku Klux Klan. In addition, Billy James Hargis and others like him have organizations which are more available. To test this proposition it would be necessary to have the membership lists of groups such as the Ku Klux Klan so that we could more accurately deal with the relationship between disorganization and membership in deviant political systems.

The position taken here is similar to that of Kai Erickson. There is a certain amount of ideological deviance in any system at any given time. Therefore, *when we attempt to account for rightist political behavior, it is necessary to keep in mind the fact that when it seems to dominate in a given area we need not assume anything other than that it was the only alternative available.*

To summarize, we explained rightist political behavior by examining two approaches. First, we attempted to account for membership in the John Birch Society by making use of measures of disorganization. It was found that the level of disorganization was strongly and consistently related to membership on a state level. The same analysis was applied on a county basis in California, and it was found that those counties in which Birchers were concentrated differed from the rest of the state in the amount of possible disorganization. Then, to apply this analysis to the census tracts within a city, we made use of a new sample composed of members of the Freedom Center. Again it was found that disorganization could account for part of the relationship. However, in explaining why a particular person joined a particular group it was necessary to shift the level of analysis. A new concept—availability—was employed to show that after one isolates predisposing conditions for membership in deviant organizations, it is necessary to examine the processes by which involvement and recruitment take place in order to explain individual involvement.

The means of dealing with the pressures that a mass society imposes on the individual are varied and can take the form of joining a religious group or a deviant political organization, therapy, and so forth. The alternatives that one has at his disposal will of course vary with such standard variables as age, sex, socioeconomic status, and race. What determines the particular group that a person will join—for example, a lower-class fundamentalist group, a political group, and so forth—has to do with the availability of a particular group when the individual has the impulse to join.

7

WHO ARE THE MEMBERS
AND WHAT DO THEY BELIEVE?

In comparing Center members to the other group of people who believe in the communist conspiracy we can better understand just how "deviant" Center members are. Are they more, or less, "radical" than other rightists in Oregon? A sample was made up of known members of conservative organizations such as the John Birch Society. The majority of the sample was composed, however, of people who had written letters to local newspapers and identified themselves as rightists, or who had written letters whose content expressed a very conservative viewpoint. Professional interviewers contacted these people in the same manner as those in the Center.

AGE OF MEMBERS

Our initial impression was that members who attended meetings and were interviewed were elderly. Why are the Centerites older than our other group of rightists? This finding is due in part to the way in which the sample was drawn. These other rightists were people who had written letters or contributed money and could be publicly identified. In contrast, the names of Centerites were not usually obtained from public records and a little over half the Center members, when questioned, said they had written to public officials. What appears, then, is a pattern of activism. Those who are most active are more likely to be young. They are more likely to write letters to public officials and business firms and radio and TV stations. However, less than half of either group write to business firms or networks.

It was found that 73 percent of Centerites were over fifty years of age.[1] Yet it is my general impression, from having worked at the Center and having interviewed those who were active in the movement, that activists tend to be younger than the rest of the members.

COMMUNITY BACKGROUNDS

Where do members of the Freedom Center come from? Rightists have been pictured by Havens as people of rural backgrounds in conflict with their urban setting.[2] Yet activities are normally centered in urban areas. The auditoriums and headquarters are in the metropolitan areas of the state and most of the members live in these areas. This means that rightism and rightist activity is an urban phenomenon. It is not surprising, then, that Havens finds rightists in cities; that is where they are in Oregon. But he raises another point, and that is that rightists, at least in the Southwest, are recent urban migrants from rural areas. Is this always the case?

We asked both Centerites and other rightists how long they had lived in the given metropolitan community and it was found that only 7 percent of Centerites and 20 percent of other rightists had been there for less than ten years. This is ample indication that the great bulk of our rightists are not recent migrants. Now, we will also want to know where they had lived before moving and where they were brought up. In response to a question which dealt with the size of the community in which the respondent had lived before he moved to the one in which he was interviewed, it was found that 60 percent of Centerites and 58 percent of other rightists had lived in a small town or rural area. In addition, 70 percent of Centerites and 70 percent of other rightists had been raised on a farm or in a small town.

What, essentially, do these facts mean? Do they mean that rightists tend to come from rural environments and cannot cope with the cultural problems presented to them in a city? Or are they meaningless? While it is true that our respondents have tended to come from rural backgrounds, we should not forget their age. Seventy-three percent of Center members are over fifty years of age, and 62 percent of our other rightists are over this mark. As any statistical abstract of the United States will indicate, much of the country was composed of small towns and rural areas forty and fifty years ago. In this light, the significance of saying that one's population of rightists came from rural areas can be questioned. Populations of non-rightists probably also came from rural areas, if they are as old as our Centerites and other groups, of rightists.

ATTITUDES TOWARD THE SOCIAL WORLD

A person's attitude toward his social surroundings may be measured in a variety of ways. Whether he thinks his opinions count for anything, whether or not he thinks others care for him, and whether or not he wishes different values were dominant, are all clues. Table 1, Question A, shows that Center members tend to believe that public officials will pay attention to their needs and desires. Fifty-nine percent of Center members agree that public officials care while 72 percent of other rightists also agree. Next, 38 percent disagree with this proposition if they are Centerites, and 26 percent of those who are among the other group of rightists disagree.

Yet, while feeling that public officials are responsive to their needs, a large amount—82 percent—of Centerites feel that they are helpless in the face of what is happening in the world today, and approximately half—58 percent—of our other rightists have similar feelings. It is interesting to note the divergence in opinion among the two groups. In Table 1, Question A, we find that more of the other rightists feel public officials care—72 percent—than do Center members—59 percent. Then, in Question B, we find this trend continues. The other rightists do not feel as ineffectual and helpless 58 —percent—as do the members of the Center—82 percent.

TABLE I

GENERALIZED ALIENATION TOWARD SOCIETY: FEELING OF HELPLESSNESS, PERSECUTION, AND DESIRE TO RETURN TO A DIFFERENT WAY OF LIFE

		(in percentages)	
		CENTERITES (N=56)	OTHER RIGHTISTS (N=53)
A. Public officials really care how people like me want things to be done.	Agree	59	72
	Disagree	38	26
	Don't Know	03	02
B. More and more I feel helpless in the face of what is happening in the world today.	Agree	82	58
	Disagree	18	40
	Don't Know	—	02
C. I think that one person can really influence what happens in society at large.	Agree	75	85
	Disagree	23	15
	Don't Know	02	—
D. If we would return to the religious, moral and family values of the past, we could solve most of today's social problems.	Agree	96	83
	Disagree	04	17
E. No one is going to care too much what happens to you when you get right down to it.	Agree	38	38
	Disagree	62	62

Note: By combining these five items into one scale with possible scores from 0-5, where 0 means that one does not feel alienated and 5 means that he is, then the respective mean scores for Centerites and Other Rightists are 2.17 and 2.70. These differences are significant at the 0.01 level.

This trend continues, Question C, where we see that more of the other rightists—85 percent—than Centerites— 75 percent—believe that it is possible for a single person to influence social outcomes. What this indicates is that our other group of rightists is more willing to believe that they play an effectual role in society, that their opinions count, and that they are not helpless.

It would seem that if a person felt himself to be an effectual and integral part of contemporary society, he would not wish to return to values of the past. We see this assumption borne out to some extent in Question D. The group of other rightists—83 percent—is somewhat less willing to return to the religious, moral and family values of the past than are Center members—96 percent. Both of these groups, however, evidence a major disenchantment with society.

In Question E we find further evidence that both groups of rightists feel somewhat insecure. The percentage of agreement with the statement that no one is going to care too much what happens to you is equal for Centerites and other rightists—38 percent.

The findings presented in the table above are consistent in that we find our other group of rightists seems to lean in a positive direction. By this we mean that they do not feel helpless, but feel that they count as individuals, and that public officials care what their opinions are. Why should this be the case? An explanation for some of the differences among these people lies in their ages. In a society that makes no provisions for the aged, we might expect to find feelings of frustration and alienation among the elderly. Their appeal to old values might thus be an appeal for a sense of stability that they now lack. Another explanation for the differences in social outlook between Center members and other rightists can also be sought in the variables of social class.

SOCIAL CLASS AND SOCIAL CLASS BACKGROUNDS

The social class of both groups of rightists was calculated by combining individual ranking on education and occupation on a seven-point scale.[3] Hollingshead's seven-fold occupational classification was employed, as was a seven-fold ranking on education. For example, if a person received an occupational ranking of "I" to receive a similar rating on education he had to have had graduate work in college. Our "scale" took the corresponding form with "I" being the highest class and "VII" the lowest. By utilizing this particular combination of variables we arrived at a social-class breakdown in which 32 percent of Centerites are in the top three classes while 56 percent of other rightists are. At the other extreme, 54 percent of Centerites are in the lowest three classes, while only 24 percent of other rightists are. Thus, our two groups of rightists are distributed at different ends of the class ladder.

The lower social classes in the United States have a mental "set" which is filled with suspicion and distrust. There are also present among the depressed classes generalized feelings of helplessness and despair.[4] But supposedly these findings apply only to those who recognize themselves as being members of these classes. Where do Centerites and other rightists perceive themselves in the class hierarchy? Respondents were given an opportunity to identify with four classes, i.e., upper class, upper-middle class, lower-middle class, or lower class. There was a definite tendency for Centerites to see themselves as lower-middle class—46 percent, while more—58 percent—of our other group of rightists identified themselves as upper-middle class. It was interesting to note that we got practically identical percentage responses for class "I" when we asked people to classify themselves, and when we classified them. For Centerites we got 3 percent in class "I" when we placed them, and 4 percent when self-rating was used. In the case of other rightists there was an identical percentage—11 percent—for both methods. As is normal[5] with self-rating techniques, the respondents place themselves higher than we would place them by taking into account their education and occupation.

Using Hollingshead's seven-fold occupational classification system, we compared the occupations of fathers and sons in our two groups. To avoid the possibility that we would be comparing fathers' and sons' occupations at different times, we took the occupation that the father had while the respondent was growing up. We compared both groups at periods of their greatest productivity, or probably highest occupational ranking. An analysis of changes for our other group of rightists indicates that 16 percent of our respondents were in the same occupational group as their fathers, 60 percent were in higher categories, and 24 percent were in lower categories.

Members of the Center were more evenly distributed than the group of other rightists. Thirty percent of them had experienced no mobility, being in the same occupational class as their father. Thirty-two percent had risen in the occupational system. Our other group of rightists appears to have fared far better; 60 percent of them were upwardly mobile, as compared to 38 percent of Centerites.

Because we have used Hollingshead's measure, we may have underestimated the downward mobility for Centerites. In Hollingshead's scheme a farm owner who has a business valued at between $20,000 and $35,000 is placed in occupational class III. He is placed in group IV if the value is between $10,000 and $20,000; and group V if the value is under $10,000. Group VI is made up of tenant farmers with a little equipment, and group VII is composed of sharecroppers. Now, half of the fathers of those interviewed were either farmers or in related occupations such as dairying or stock farming. We categorized *all* farmers as belonging to Hollingshead's group V, since complete data was often not available and we did not wish to bias the interpretation. In group V the income and value of the farm is under $10,000. This would be a very small farm, immediately above the level of tenant and sharecropper. By comparing the father's education to his occupation it seemed unlikely that any of the fathers involved would have fallen into group VI or VII. From the description supplied, some of them were obviously wealthy ranchers. However, we placed all of them in the lowest possible category. Again, this does not deal with the historical fact that farming was once an occupation of a large minority of American families, and was not considered to be at the lower end of the occupational scale. The security and recognition that

Centerites may have experienced while growing up has disappeared as they have become older. This again would create a predisposition for feelings of status anxiety.

FAMILY STRUCTURE

A Center worker once mentioned the fact that the Center received so many "deceased notices" from the post office that it was hard to keep their files up to date. She said that sometimes notices came into the Center at the rate of one a day. There is no doubt that the people who belong to the Center are clustered at the top of the age distribution in the state. These factors should be reflected in marital status of Center members, for if many of them are old there should be a large number of widows and widowers.

My acquaintance with many of the people interviewed allowed me to secure most of the needed information. No information was available for 6 percent of them, but 44 percent were married and living with their spouses, 26 percent were widowed, 3 percent divorced, and 21 percent were single.

Thus, we cannot attribute rightism to a breakdown in the family for it seems in many cases to be a family affair. Both the husbands and wives whom we interviewed participated in the various activities. They came to meetings together, they listened to radio programs with each other, and they discussed issues together. This does not, however, preclude the assumption that rightist activities occur because there is a breakdown in the *extended* family. These people are elderly and those who once had children no longer have them to take care of. (In addition, those respondents who still have children living at home have not been able to involve their children in rightist activities.) They have free time. A spouse, unless he or she is bedridden or an invalid, does not tend to hamper the activities of these people. This is also reflected in the work in which Centerites involve themselves. Out of a total of 68 persons for whom data was available we found that 47 percent said they worked, 22 percent were retired, 26 percent were housewives, and five percent were unclassifiable. The figure of 47 percent working could be reduced further because this also includes those who work part-time.

One elderly man said, in response to the question as to why he got involved in rightist activities, "Why, it gives me something to do!" I expect that similar reasons are at work among other Center members. To be sure, there is a certain ideological predisposition necessary, but one must also have the time. An impression that I got from talking to several people was that they were involved in many things. One woman said, "I work a little at the Center, but I have so many things to do. I have my church work, and then I go to other meetings."

The meetings, as we have noted, are also social gatherings of a sort. People meet with friends, arrive with them, and leave with them. When people came to the Center to work during the Goldwater-Miller campaign, they brought their lunches and stayed the whole day to work and talk to their friends. For people who have limited primary group ties, some means must be found to reaffirm and strengthen those available. The Center provided a focal point around which friendships could be built and strengthened. The significance, then, of the marital status of Center members is that it provides a "predisposition" for these people to involve themselves in activity.

RELIGIOUS AFFILIATION AND RELIGIOUS BELIEFS

The Center's publications and public meetings are dominated by religious themes and rhetoric. In an open-ended question which asked respondents what problems in America they were particularly concerned or worried about, an overwhelming number of Center members specified that it was

"Godless communism." They did not just say communism or socialism, but specified the godless nature of communism. The other group of rightists did not do this. Their answers did not include religious rhetoric or terminology. In addition, a question was asked: "What sort of person is likely to be Communist?" Centerites tended to respond in terms of: "People who are Godless. . . . People who don't believe in God. . . . Irreligious people. . . ." Other rightists were more likely to respond in non-religious terms.

Table 2 lets us see how Centerites differ from other rightists in religious beliefs. In Part A of Table 2, we find both groups responding in the "expected" direction, with 98 percent of Center members and 86 percent of the other rightists expressing an unqualified belief in God. This compared to the National Sample taken by Gallup, indicates that our other group of rightists "deviates" from the regional pattern. This could be due to the fact that the Gallup organization was supposedly sampling across classes, while our other group of rightists tends to be concentrated in the upper dimensions of our class structure.

Where belief in a life after death is concerned, we find that it is the Centerite who is likely to diverge from the common beliefs. In Part B, we see that 91 percent of Center members, 72 percent of other rightists, and 63 percent of the Pacific Coast sample, believe in a life after death. One of the reasons for finding Centerites professing such a belief is their religious affiliation. Over one-third of Center members belong to Baptist denominations—34 percent. On the other hand, almost a third—32 percent—of our group of other rightists are members of either the Episcopalian, Unitarian, Presbyterian, or Congregational church. Their patterns of church membership are related to the social classes to which they belong. The other rightists concentrate in the upper-class churches; and the Center members, being from lower social classes, tend to be found in churches with low prestige.

The fact that 78 percent of Center members believe that some people will be punished by God in the next life while

TABLE II

ATTITUDES TOWARD SPECIFIC RELIGIOUS BELIEFS AND VIEWS OF THE BIBLE

	(in percentages)		
	CENTERITES	OTHER RIGHTISTS	PACIFIC COAST
A. Believe in God?			
Yes	98	86	93
No	—	06	01
Not Sure	—	06	06
Qualifies Yes	02	02	—
T	100%	100%	100%
B. Believe in life after death?			
Yes	91	72	63
No	05	15	14
Not Sure	04	13	23
T	100%	100%	100%
C. Believe that in the next life some people will be punished by God?			
Does Not Apply*	05	17	
Yes	73	40	
No	16	30	
Not Sure	06	13	
T	100%	100%	
N	56	53	
D. Views on the Bible			
1. The Bible is God's word and all it says is true.	69	23	
2. The Bible was written by men inspired by God, and its moral and religious teachings are true, but because the writers were men, it contains some human errors.	20	51	
3. The Bible is a valuable book which teaches symbolically basic moral and religious truths.	07	20	
4. The Bible is a valuable book because it was written by wise and good men, but God had nothing to do with it.	02	02	
5. The Bible was written by men who lived so long ago that it is of little value today.	02	—	
6. No answer.	—	04	
T	100%	100%	

Source: Leo Rosten (ed.), **A Guide to the Religions of America** (New York: Simon and Schuster, 1955), pp. 237-38. The figures he reports are from the 1944 Gallup poll for the Pacific Coast states: California, Oregon, and Washington.

* This refers to those people who, in the previous question, Part B, said that they did not believe in a life after death.

only 40 percent of other rightists believe this (Part C) is a
further consequence of class membership and denominational
affiliation. Center members believe that the Bible is God's
word and all it says is true—69 percent. On the other hand,
only a few—23 percent—of the other rightists believe in a
literal interpretation of everything the Bible says.

Seventy-two percent of our Center members belong to
conservative denominations and only 30 percent of other
rightists do. But our other rightists are not concentrated in
liberal denominations. A few more—9 percent—said that
they were Protestants but did not belong or go to any specific
denomination. What these last two figures indicate is that
probably 24 percent of our group of other rightists is unchurched. The assumption is made that if a person does not
profess any affiliation or simply calls himself a Protestant,
religion does not play a major role in the life of the respondent.

POLITICAL AFFILIATION AND VOTING

During the weeks before the presidential election of 1964,
the Center displayed a large sign saying: "State Headquarters,
Citizens for Goldwater-Miller." Inside pamphlets relating to
the campaign were laid out on the tables. A golden bucket
with a ladle was present for contributions to the Goldwater
campaign, and one could buy a canned soft drink called
"Goldwater," and other trinkets and souvenirs of the campaign. The Center was, in short, dedicated to the task of
trying to get Goldwater elected. But were all of the people
present Republicans, and did all Center members vote for
Goldwater?

It is interesting that although an extremely high percentage of both groups voted for Goldwater—84 percent and
92 percent—Centerites were not as likely to vote for him as
the other rightists. This could be due to what Lazarsfeld has

termed cross-pressures.[6] If for the Center group we combined the categories of "Did Not Vote" and "Other Candidate," the percentages for the two groups would be almost identical. (See Table A.6 in the Appendix.) Another partial answer can be sought in "crossover." In a question which asked what party the respondent belonged to it was found that a sizable proportion of Centerites call themselves Democrats and independents. It was from this group that the Johnson votes came. Ninety-two percent of them initially identified themselves as Republicans and carried through with this identification at the polls.

Is it possible to vote Democratic, and/or identify oneself as a Democrat, yet still be considered a rightist? Apparently so, if we examine these people's beliefs about communism and the amount of communist influence in our government. These people believe in a communist conspiracy.

Centerites are quite positive in their belief that Communists have infiltrated the government. Forty-four percent of them feel that there is a great deal of communist influence in government, while 38 percent of the other rightists feel the same way. If we compare the total percentages for belief in communist influence in government we find that 98 percent of Centerites and 96 percent of the other rightists believe there is at least some communist influence in government. Thus, even though some of the Centerites did not vote, and/or some voted for President Johnson, they believe communism is a current danger in government.

They do not view this danger as slight. Sixty-eight percent of Center members, as opposed to 58 percent of other rightists, believe that there is a great deal of danger to the country because of communist influence in government. Ninety-eight percent of Freedom Center members and 96 percent of other rightists believe that there is at least some danger to the country.

Centerites diverge thirty percentage points from the group of other rightists in seeing a great deal of communist influence in American schools and colleges. However, the combined percentages reveal that 98 percent of Centerites and all of the other rightists believe there is a communist influence in the schools.

These findings seem to indicate that belief in a communist conspiracy is somewhat divorced from ordinary political concerns. By this we do not mean that rightists are not concerned about what goes on in Washington, but that some of them do not see the presidential elections as relating to the issues that concern the rightist. In other words, it did not matter to some of the Centerites whether or not they voted for Johnson or Goldwater. These candidates were not related to the issues as some people saw them. For instance, after the election we questioned several people at length about the future of conservatism, and asked whether or not they saw the election as marking the doom of conservative movements. Instead of explaining why Goldwater had not been elected, Centerites began to talk about the relationship between religion and conservatism. "The only thing," said one woman, "that can save this country is for the people to turn to God and the Bible."

Centerites overwhelmingly believe that there has been a decay of morals in our country—94 percent. Other rightists also believe quite strongly that there has been a breakdown in morals—80 percent. Those people given in-depth interviews consistently expressed greater concern about moral issues than they did about political issues. It is in this sense, then, that the rightist might not view a presidential campaign as "significant" unless "moral" issues were at stake.

As has been indicated by Lipset et al., people turn out to vote when they have a vested interest in the outcome of the election.[7] By virtue of their age, many Centerites fit this criterion. Seventy-three percent of them are over the age of fifty and their incomes are low. They worry about how they are going to pay medical bills. A significant proportion of Centerites—32 percent—believe that the government ought to help people get medical aid, while only 19 percent of other rightists believe that the government ought to provide aid. This percentage difference is due partly to the fact that 73 percent of other rightists are over fifty. Another reason is the comparative income of the two groups. The Centerites have much lower reported incomes than do the other rightists.

Some Centerites—32 percent—are willing to have the government provide medical care, something which directly concerns some of them. Their attitude toward other government-provided benefits is different. Normally, if the legislation helps people other than themselves—for example, civil rights, welfare reform—they are opposed to it.

Center members are more willing—45 percent—to have the government aid the black in his search for fair treatment in jobs and housing than are other rightists—28 percent. However, Centerites are not consistent in their attitudes regarding civil rights. Centerites do not want the government to become involved in desegregating the schools—82 percent opposed. Centerites are more likely—42 percent—to believe that the federal government should help people find jobs than are the other rightists—13 percent.

At first glance these findings may appear to be contradictory. They are not. What the above evidence indicates is that the Centerites "identify" with the plight of the black in his search for housing and employment. It would appear that the Centerite has placed himself in the blacks' position and translated the question to: "Should the federal government help people who are not getting fair treatment in jobs and housing?" Almost exactly the same number of people—45 percent as opposed to 42 percent—believe that the government should help everyone get a job who wants one. (An examination of the crossover for these two items shows that the same people are responding positively, which gives further weight to this assumption.) Secondly, we find a consistency among the other group of rightists. They are opposed to aiding blacks in their search for jobs and homes—70 percent—opposed to desegregation of schools—78 percent—and opposed to the federal government trying to find jobs for everybody who wants a job—87 percent opposed—while many Centerites favor government help—42 percent approve. As we have noted, our other group of rightists has a higher reported yearly income than Center members. They have jobs; they are secure; they are younger, and many are still at the peak of their earning power. This is probably why they do not believe that the government needs to help people get jobs. Centerites, then, exhibit an apparent ambivalence regarding matters of civil rights, but this is clarified when we examine their relative economic position and compare their responses to those of another group of rightists.

Various writers have pointed out some of the non-logical patterning of rightist beliefs. While believing—42 percent—that the government ought to aid people to find jobs, Centerites believe that we should return to an age where individual initiative is foremost, and Center members and the other rightists are almost totally in agreement with the notion that people should stand on their own feet.

IDEOLOGY

If a person belongs to a rightist organization, what does this mean in terms of the ideology he espouses? The Right in the United States has often been viewed as a monolithic and homogeneous whole. Rightists, as rightists, are supposed to subscribe to a dogma which has as its central theme a belief in the communist conspiracy. Pamphlets and tracts published by rightist groups equate everything to the left of them as suspect. This is evidenced by their assumption that liberalism, socialism, and communism can all be drawn out of the same hat.

According to Durkheimian theory, if a group is a stable ongoing organization it has a common core of values, and it has some ritual whereby it periodically reaffirms its faith in these values. The membership of the organization is in many respects a transient population. Yet Center members have similar belief patterns. It appears that the "group" of Centerites believes in a common core of values, without benefit of a ritual system such as meetings and rallies. Although some of the members get together to work and faithfully attend the few meetings that are still held, they do not constitute the majority of the membership. What seems to happen is essentially this: there is an alternative ritual supplied by other rightist organizations and rightist radio speakers. One of the distinguishing characteristics of the Center members is their belief in and adherence to a fundamentalistic religious dogma. This, coupled with their anti-communism, finds constant support through the medium of the radio.

One of the things noted in the open-ended questionnaire was what programs these people listened to and discussed with others. Every one of the fifteen respondents I contacted listened faithfully to such radio programs as those of Billy James Hargis, Carl McIntire, Richard Cotton, and Walter Huss. All of these programs espouse an anti-communist ideology heavily laden with religious terminology. Again, every one of the respondents received mailings from these programs, as well as other rightist organizations. Some received literature from Gerald L. K. Smith, the *Cross and the Flag;* some from Alexander Schiffner in Spokane, Washington, the *Prophetic Herald;* some from Myron C. Fagan, director of the Cinema Educational Guild in Hollywood, California. Some received materials from Cotton, Smoot, Hargis, McIntire, and others connected with rightist organizations and programs. My visits to people's homes were always marked by their attempts to give me such literature—books, magazines, pamphlets, and numerous tracts. Every household I went into, and several which the professional interviewers went into, had a superfluity of materials on every conceivable subject that the right is interested in—mental health, fluoridation, civil rights, the right to bear arms, and so on. It is by this means that the ritual is supplied and beliefs are reaffirmed. My impression is that the people we talked to felt that they were doing their part simply because they had tried to give this material to me and to the interviewers. A full mailbox signifies to them that they are helping to fight communism. This ritual is further strengthened by the fact that they talk to other people about what they read and what they listen to.

An overwhelming proportion of Centerites—86 percent —and other rightists believe that America is just about a perfect society. Sixty-four percent of Center members and 62 percent of other rightists say that they are for their country right or wrong. Center members believe that the worst danger to real Americanism during the last fifty years has come from foreign ideas and agitators, while a lesser percentage—57 percent—of other rightists feel this way. This finding can probably be attributed to the fact that Centerites tend to come from lower socioeconomic groups. This is in line with the findings of many other studies and especially the interpretations that Lipset makes in his "Working-Class Authoritarianism." As he notes, if liberalism is defined in noneconomic terms, then working-class people are intolerant.[8] That members of the Center are intolerant because of their lower-class position seems to be true. Let us see if this intolerance of Centerites can be described as authoritarian.

First, what do we mean by authoritarianism? We use this term to refer to an individual's unwillingness to accept alternative proposals or solutions for an issue, to look for the easiest solution to any problem, and not to accept any deviance. As we have seen, many Centerites are members of denominations which are chiliastically oriented, and this finds its reflection in a Centerite's stance on political issues.

The question was asked as to whether the compromising of principles leads to nothing but destruction. Eighty-six percent of both Centerites and other rightists were unwilling to compromise any of their principles. On the basis of this information it would appear that we cannot attribute authoritarianism only to Centerites, nor take religion in this case as a distinguishing mark between the two groups. But the question of whether or not to compromise with political opponents is to be guilty of appeasement, appears to be more meaningful. Whereas the former question does not necessarily relate to the political realm, this one does, and we find that Centerites feel more strongly (thirteen percentage points difference) about the matter than the other rightists. The relationship between certain religious and authoritarian political beliefs has also been noted by Lipset.

Many observers have called attention to a connection between low social status and fundamentalist or chiliastic religion. This suggests that extremist religion is a product of the same social forces that sustain authoritarian political attitudes.[9]

How do Center members fare on other items that can be taken as a mark of authoritarianism? Both groups believe that obedience and respect for authority are the most important virtues that children should learn (Table 4, Question A). Ten percent more (83 percent as opposed to 93 percent) Center members than other rightists agree with this statement. In addition, both groups think that the public schools should increase the teaching of respect for authority. Ninety-eight percent of Centerites and 90 percent of other rightists believe this. Although the comparison can not be a rigorous one, Gerhard Lenski reports data in *The Religious Factor* that allows us to get a perspective on the results we report. He indicates that the percentages of his sample who value intellectual autonomy above obedience vary by class. The data reported for white Protestants who value intellectual autonomy runs as follows: upper-middle class, 90 percent; lower-middle class, 86 percent; upper-working class, 66 percent; lower-working class, 48 percent.[10] It must be noted that our respondents were not really provided with a choice. They were not asked to choose between intellectual autonomy and obedience as the most desired traits for children; they had to respond in terms of the one. But they responded on two questions in such a high positive direction for authority that we can see that our group seems to be more rigid than Lenski's sample in their valuing of authority.

TABLE III

ELEMENTS OF AUTHORITARIANISM AS DEFINED BY ATTITUDES OF CENTERITES AND OTHER RIGHTISTS

		(in percentages) CENTERITES (N=56)	OTHER RIGHTISTS (N=53)
A. Obedience and respect for authority are the most important virtues children should learn.	Agree	93	83
	Disagree	07	15
	Don't Know	—	02
B. We should increase the teaching of respect for authority in the schools.	Agree	98	90
	Disagree	02	08
	Don't Know	—	02
C. There is usually only one right way to do anything.	Agree	68	38
	Disagree	32	62
D. In this complicated world of ours the only way we can know what is going on is to rely upon leaders or experts who can be trusted.	Agree	79	47
	Disagree	21	51
	Don't Know	—	02
E. Sex crimes such as rape and attacks on children deserve more than mere imprisonment: such criminals ought to be publicly whipped or worse.	Agree	74	57
	Disagree	24	37
	Don't Know	02	06
F. Homosexuals are hardly better than criminals and ought to be severely punished.	Agree	73	43
	Disagree	23	53
	Don't Know	04	04
G. People can be divided into two distinct classes: the weak and the strong.	Agree	68	53
	Disagree	32	47
H. Life is primarily a matter of struggle for survival.	Agree	68	62
	Disagree	32	38

Note: By combining these items into one scale with possible scores from 0-8, where 0 means that one does not exhibit any authoritarian tendencies and 8 means that he does, then the respective mean scores for Centerites and Other Rightists are 6.1 and 4.7. These differences are significant at the 0.01 level.

A discussion of question C of Table 3 should be preceded by a quotation from Lipset.

The proposition that the lack of a rich, complex frame of reference is the vital variable which connects low status and a predisposition toward extremism does not necessarily suggest that the lower strata will be authoritarian; it implies that, other things being equal, they will choose the least complex alternative.[11]

This is what this part of our table indicates. Sixty-eight

percent of Center members say that there is only one right way to do anything, while 30 percent less of our other rightists agree with this statement.

Right wing politics in the United States, Peronism in Argentina, and the fascism of the Third Reich and of Italy have all had some things in common. The followers of these movements give their unquestioning support to a dominant leader and the movements are characterized by an authoritarian structure, strong nationalistic orientation, and an ideology which blames all of the followers' and the country's troubles on foreign elements, ideas, and people. But do the various members of these groups all give their unquestioning support to one leader? Does education seem to make a difference? It would appear so, for in Table 4, Question D, we find a divergence between Centerites and other rightists. Seventy-nine percent of Center members believe that in this complicated world of ours the only way we can know what is going on is to rely upon leaders or experts who can be trusted. Over half—51 percent—of other rightists want to make their own decisions; they balk at trusting all leaders.

Who are the leaders to whom these groups give their loyalty? When we asked the question "Would you tell me someone who, in your opinion, is a great American? Someone who is living, or recently lived," the other group of rightists was likely to name such people as Senator Taft, ex-President Hoover, and of course, Barry Goldwater. Centerites also named some of the same men, but with a slightly different orientation. There was more of a tendency to name religious personages and radical rightists, not "conservatives." By this we mean that we would call Eisenhower and Barry Goldwater conservatives, but men like Governor Wallace, Carl McIntire, and Gerald L. K. Smith—all of whom were identified as great Americans by Centerites—radical rightists. Most Centerites identified four people as great Americans: Barry Goldwater, Douglas MacArthur, Herbert Hoover, and Billy Graham. They also placed people like General Walker,

Richard Cotton, Oral Roberts, Ronald Reagan, Edward Mc-
Birnie, Strom Thurmond, J. Edgar Hoover, and Billy Hargis
in the category of great Americans. All of these men could
be characterized as strong leaders.

As Theodore Adorno and his associates point out in *The
Authoritarian Personality,* one mark of an authoritarian is his
inability or unwillingness to accept deviance in any form.[12]
Questions E and F allow us to see what attitudes Centerites
have toward sexual deviance. In the first we can see that 74
percent of Center members believe that sex crimes, such as
rape and attacks on children, deserve more than mere im-
prisonment; that such criminals ought to be publicly whipped
or worse. A smaller percentage—57 percent—of other rightists are willing to agree that sex criminals ought to be publicly whipped. A corresponding question, Question F, shows that
there is still a wide margin between the responses of Center
members and other rightists. Seventy-three percent of Centerites believe that homosexuals are hardly better than criminals and ought to be severely punished. Forty-three percent of
other rightists are in agreement. Thus there appears to be
strong evidence for the proposition that Centerites are more
likely than other rightists to be authoritarian personalities.

As we noted before, the authoritarian personality tends
to view phenomena as belonging to one of two classes.
Things are either white or black; they are not gray. Centerites' views of people also take this same shape. In Question G,
68 percent of Center members say that people can be divided
into two distinct classes—the weak and the strong—and fifty-
three percent of other rightists say the same thing. The final
question, H, deals with the same attitude. If life is viewed
as a struggle for survival, the assumption is that the fittest
will survive and the weak will succumb. An identical percentage of Centerites (the same people) see people as belonging
to one of two classes and life as a struggle for survival—68
percent. Sixty-two percent of other rightists agree that life
is to be viewed in terms of conflict.

How do our Centerites compare to people who have

been identified as authoritarian personalities? Howard Becker, in an article that deals with interviews with German officials under the Nazis, outlines criteria for the "regimented German official." Certain criteria were isolated for this particular type, among which were these: 1) an unquestioning although not necessarily intense nationalism; 2) an articulate belief in the beneficence of rigid authoritarianism; 3) an acceptance of and gratification in the role of serving higher authority; 4) a highly developed work ethic; 5) a transference of decision-making powers to superiors; 6) a tendency to think of deviant behavior as virtually criminal; and one or two similar criteria.[13]

Although we do not have adequate data to see whether Centerites conform to all of these criteria, we can examine how their attitudes relate to some of them.[14] First, the expression of an unquestioning, though not necessarily intense nationalism, leads us back to 86 percent of Centerites who feel that America is the perfect society and are for their country, right or wrong—64 percent. This implies that Center members have both an unquestioning *and* an intensely nationalistic attitude. Their ethnocentric position is further highlighted by the fact that they see the real danger to Americanism as coming from foreign ideas and agitators—90 percent. In this case, then, they are different from Nazi officials in that they are both unquestioningly and intensely nationalistic.

The second criterion, an articulate belief in the beneficence of rigid authoritarianism, was found in Centerites. Ninety-three percent expressed a belief that the most important virtue a child could learn was obedience and respect for authority. This in turn was reflected in their belief that there was only one right way to do something—68 percent. If a person adheres to both of these beliefs we may say that authoritarianism becomes good because it solves problems. It is the simplest approach to things. Intellectual autonomy in children poses problems; obedience does not. Multiple solutions to any social problem present ambiguities and discomforts; one solution does not. In this sense, we may say that Centerites conform to the second criterion.

Unfortunately there were no questions asked of respondents which would allow us to deal adequately with the third criterion; but for the fourth, an acceptance of an exppression of a highly-developed work ethic, there were. A total of 94 percent of Centerites believed that people were wasting their money and not saving it. Seventy-five percent agreed with the statement that to be respected a man must have worked hard for some important goal, and 73 percent believed that thrift and industriousness were the most important traits a man could develop.

The fact that 79 percent of Centerites believe that the world is complicated and therefore the only way one can know what is going on is to rely upon leaders or experts, seems to support the fifth criterion given by Becker. This criterion was the willingness of the Nazi official to transfer all final decision-making power to superiors and to accept this decision because it was "right."

The regimented German Nazi official whom Becker described was unwilling to accept any form of deviance. There was a strong tendency among these officials to view non-conformist behavior as virtually criminal. The Centerite feels essentially the same way for he is willing to state—73 percent —that homosexuals are hardly better than criminals and ought to be severely punished. The assumption that Centerites conform to the sixth criterion—that deviance is not acceptable—was also supported by their belief that there is only one right way to do something—68 percent—that one cannot compromise principles—86 percent—and that if one compromises with his political opponents he is guilty of appeasement—73 percent. Eighty-two percent of them believe that a group which tolerates too much difference of opinion among its own members cannot last long. Only 45 percent of the other group of rightists adopts this position. Consequently, we can say that Centerites exhibit another tendency to be like the regimented Nazi official described by Becker.

Centerites exhibit the traits of an authoritarian personality. Like the regimented Nazi official they see things in terms of black and white. Yet all rightists cannot be put in the same basket. Our other group of rightists, composed of people who support the Liberty Amendment, are Birch Society members or Manion supporters and come from an upper dimension of the class scale. Our Centerites do not. Partly as a result of their economic situation and partly as a result of their adherence to chiliastic religions, the Centerites exhibit an unwavering authoritarian stance.

Part Three

THE CAREER OF
A RADICAL RIGHTIST

8

THE CAREER OF A RADICAL RIGHTIST

Howard S. Becker in *Outsiders* views deviancy as a process, and implies that the deviant learns a "career" in the same way that another man learns to become a lawyer or a university professor. There is progression from initial commitment to the assuming of the final position.[1] It may at first seem unnatural to view one's membership in a rightist organization in the light of a model that will encompass the activities of narcotics addicts, thieves, and homosexuals. But, like the homosexual or narcotic addict, the radical rightist learns to become a member of a group which is not in the mainstream of American society. I do not intend to imply that a rightist is deviant in the sense that is ordinarily meant. Becker's model is used because it is a useful and discerning way to show how groups of people become isolated from the dominant society, and select ways of dealing with frustrations and concerns that are different from those of other people.

The main steps in the deviant career are: 1) the commission of a nonconforming act; 2) the experience of being caught and publicly labeled as a deviant; 3) support of similar deviance; and 4) movement into an organized deviant group in which the deviant is supplied with a rationale for his behavior by the other members of the group.[2] Becker sees this applying to a marijuana user.[3] An individual is encouraged by his friends to try marijuana. If he likes it and receives support for his habit, he continues. He may be caught and charged with illegal possession of marijuana and labeled by the general public as a "pot head." This is the second stage. After being labeled as deviant by the general community he may find that his deviant act will bring rewards (stage three) only with people who smoke marijuana. Thus he "joins" their group (stage four) and finds that he is secure. No one any longer attacks his behavior or labels it "queer." In fact, his new group has a rationale which explains that it is the rest of the society which is deviant.

The same thing happens to the radical rightist. First, there is the commission of a deviant act. How do we explain why the person committed the initial act? Becker says that people have usually thought of the nonconforming act as motivated, but that motivation need not play a major role.

Unintended acts of deviance can probably be accounted for relatively simply. They imply an ignorance of the existence of the rule, or the fact that it was applicable in this case, or to this particular person.[4]

Becker goes on to examine some of the traditional explanations for deviance and says:

Instead of asking why deviants want to do things that are disapproved of, we might better ask why conventional people do not follow through on the deviant impulses they have.[5]

His conclusion is that "normal" people go through a process in which they become more and more committed to the dominant society. As a person acquires more education and a better job he becomes more "committed" to the society, and has more to lose by commission of a deviant act. He can lose his reputation in the community, his job, and possibly the respect of his family. Thus, there must be factors that weaken society's hold on the deviant. These are not necessarily factors which lead to the commission of the deviant act, but they are what can be called "predisposing factors."

PREDISPOSING CONDITIONS

One of the things of concern when dealing with predisposing conditions is a person's social class. As will be recalled, the social class of Centerites was calculated by combining individual ranking on education and occupation on a seven-point scale.[6] It was found that Centerites tended to come from the bottom class. Fifty-four percent were found in the last three classes, and only 12 percent in the first two. This is in marked contrast to the state and city in which these people live. The state has one of the highest ratios of any state of college graduates to total population, and the city's population is concentrated in the first three classes of Hollinghead's occupational scale.[7] Consequently the Centerites find themselves in a society which is decidedly middle-class and they are partly isolated from the dominant society.

Related to the question of the social class of radical rightists is the question of how far they have moved—up or down—in our class system. The present occupation of Centerites was compared with their father's occupation at similar periods, i.e., at the peak of their occupational careers. The conclusion was that these rightists had not moved up in the class system and had, in a significant number of cases, fallen lower. (Sixty-two percent were either downwardly mobile, or experienced no mobility.) Our occupational system had expanded, leaving these people behind.[8]

As was noted in our earlier description of a typical meeting, these people are old. Seventy-three percent of the respondents were over fifty years of age. By virtue of their age, many of these people had retired, or held only part-time jobs. The dominant society has to some extent, lost control over their activities. The fact that the larger society does not control them in the sense that it can withhold jobs was illustrated by the responses to a question which dealt with their employment. Seventy-three percent of these people were either retired, unemployed, or self-employed.

Another predisposing condition is that many radical rightists are at the end of their family life-cycles and thus have the leisure time to devote to outside activities. One elderly gentleman when questioned about his membership in this organization replied: "Why, it gives me *something to do!* All people my age ought to get interested in this thing and do something, instead of sitting around." This indicates rather dramatically one very important function of the group. The people who were members of the Center were, in most cases, using the Center's activities for social rather than political reasons. In fact, one can say that communism per se was not the real concern of these people. They were interested in personal integration; it just happened that this group had been originally founded to fight communism.

Related to this condition of integration is the marital status of Center members. Fifty percent of these rightists were either widowed, single, or divorced. Because they are at the upper end of the age distribution and because they do not have to spend time in the home caring for children, they devote their energies to political activities. Another predisposing factor that is related to age and family structure is the elderly person's role in our society. People are neither socialized to deal with these roles in terms of maintaining extended family ties, nor is it expected that they provide economic and psychological support of elderly family members, nor are the elderly themselves prepared to deal with their roles. A reason why age might be a predisposing condition to a deviant career was reflected in an old man's response to the question, "What problems are you concerned with today in our society?" His response was: "No respect. . . . Young kids are always calling me 'Pop.'"

That the Centerite feels isolated and cut off from the rest of the society can be illustrated by reference to Table 1 in Chapter 7. There it can be seen that there is an overwhelming tendency to feel helpless and ineffectual together with a desire to escape into the past to solve one's problems. Centerites react to their positions of low status and ineffectuality in dealing with their social environment. There is a strong tendency to take an authoritarian stance in dealing with deviance of any kind and it is evident that respect for authority and the need for it are predominant.

Another predisposing condition has to do with the relationship between dwelling area and behavior. It is true that we find many types of deviants concentrated in certain areas of any large city. The delinquent is one example. In the delinquent's case we can say that his physical surroundings are both facilitating and predisposing conditions for his delinquency. The predisposing conditions are poverty in the most general sense and, perhaps, broken homes; while the facilitating conditions are the lack of educational, recreational, and vocational opportunities, and rejection by the middle-class society. But some other factor must operate to explain why everybody in a given area is not a delinquent. One important condition and facilitating factor is the gang. Here other adolescents who come from the same social background meet and derive mutual physical and emotional support. Friendship matrices can pull an adolescent youth from a lower-class broken home into a delinquent gang. What is the situation for the rightist?

It was seen in Chapter 6 that neither a measure of social disorganization nor social status could account for location of Center members' residences. (There was a slight, though not significant, tendency for Center members to come from those areas of the city marked by low social status *and* high social disorganization.) This meant that area of residence per se could not be advanced as an explanation of why someone became a rightist. As was the case with the delinquent, we would have to explain why everybody else in the area did not become a rightist. An answer to this question leads us in the direction of the other major reason a person might become a rightist, the "facilitating conditions."

FACILITATING CONDITIONS

The major facilitating condition is the same for the rightist as it is for the delinquent. It is a friendship matrix. The lower-class adolescent finds this group of friends in the area in which he lives, but this is not the case with our radical rightists. We find them scattered throughout the city, but pulled together by previously existing bonds. First, the members of this group were concentrated in four fundamentalist churches—72 percent. Membership in these churches existed prior to membership in the Center. Second, during the time the interviewers were in the field, many of the respondents contacted one another to find out if their friends were also being contacted. The possibility exists that some of these friendships may have developed after the person became a member of the organization, but another factor was at work to make me believe that most friendships were prior friendships. In an examination of the location of the 266 Freedom Center members' residences, we found that there tended to be clusters. A high percentage lived in and around the area where the Center was located. In addition, three or four members would be found on the same street and block in another part of town. A third facilitating condition for some people was the "availability" of activities. Twenty-five percent of Centerites were found to live in the same census tract or that adjacent to the one in which the Center was located. Members were able to get to the Center and participate in the activities. Finally, at all of the many meetings we attended, people always greeted one another, inquired after family members, and sometimes discussed other activities in which they were mutually involved. In addition, when we went to one of the members' homes, it was not uncommon to have another member drop in. Friendship patterns were an important variable in understanding how the Center was organized.

To summarize, then, the main predisposing and facilitating conditions for becoming a radical rightist take the following pattern.

PREDISPOSING CONDITIONS

1. *Social Class*—The Centerites tended to be both down-wardly mobile, and concentrated in the lower social classes.

2. *Age*—With increasing age and consequent retire-ment comes the leisure time necessary to engage in social and political activities.

3. *Family Status*—Many Centerites were at the end of their family life-cycles, and/or were single, widowed, or divorced. They were bound to a small family unit or were without a spouse and had the time to en-gage in activities outside of the home.

4. *General Attitudes*—It was noted that many of the Centerites experienced feeling of alienation coupled with authoritarian leanings.

5. *Dwelling Area*—Living in an area characterized by high rates of social disorganization and a low social status had a slight tendency to explain membership.

FACILITATING CONDITIONS

1. *Friendship Matrices*—Membership in fundamental-ist churches where members knew one another was a causal factor in determining the consequent friend-ship patterns in the Center. And this accounted for the process by which people were made aware of and recruited to the Center.

2. *Availability*—It was noted that the members' homes were located in such a fashion that the Center was easily accessible to them. Other organizations of a similar political nature did not intervene geographic-ally in their choice of an organization to join.

What this means is that *a person who is predisposed to join an organization will join one which is similar to his ideol-ogy, i.e., authoritarian, and which is available to him, i.e., is convenient, and there, when the impetus to join comes.*

Now that we have dealt with some of the predisposing and

facilitating conditions let us return to our rightist's career. Our rightist takes the first step in the deviant career, i.e., the commission of a non-conforming act, because he is predisposed to do so and because he is able to do so. But what is the deviant act? In the case of a delinquent it is easy to pick out the initial act which could take forms such as breaking and entering or vandalism, for example.

What is the counterpart in the case of a rightist? The non-conformist act may take the form of labeling Eisenhower or a Supreme Court justice as tools of the Communists. One may write to his local newspaper and say that an established senator is "giving aid and comfort to the communist cause" because of his votes. Or, one may warn mothers, as did the Center, of impending dangers.

Did you know that CUB SCOUTS—boys as young as nine years old—are being TRAINED inside the Cub Scout organization to COEXIST WITH COMMUNISTS? Did you know, DEN MOTHERS ARE SUPPOSED TO TEACH THE CUBS UNDER THEIR CONTROL THAT COEXISTENCE WITH A DEADLY ENEMY WHO IS DETERMINED TO ENSLAVE OUR NATION BRINGS PEACE WITH JUSTICE?

Exert every influence you can to PREVENT any sort of UN flag being flown this year in Portland—or in your city—and by all means oppose any attempt to select some innocent young girl as MISS UNITED NATIONS.[9]

If a person does any of these or similar things, he is committing a non-conforming or deviant act.

What, then, is "deviant?" Quite simply, deviance is what people decide to call deviance. The responses of the larger community must be considered, then, when we deal with the second step in the career of a deviant, the experience of being caught and publicly labeled a "pot head" or "junkie" by the community. The person who labels Eisenhower a dupe, Chief Justice Earl Warren as a "conscious tool," and says that the Cub Scout organization is subversive, is also labeled by his community. He is called a "nut," a "crank," or, sometimes, a radical rightist. The labeling reinforces the deviant behavior

174

to the extent that it gives the person status as a deviant. He enjoys recognition and response which he did not evoke before, however negative it might be. At one meeting a woman interrupted the speaker to tell how she had been singled out by her neighbors as a rightist. Giggling she went on to describe how twice her garbage can had been tipped upside down on her back porch.

In the third step, support of similar deviance, the person, after having committed the deviant act, will continue to "deviate" as long as he can find reinforcement that he likes. The adolescent finds that his repeated acts of violence give him a new status among his peer group. He is a person with a recognized status among people with similar desires and frustrations. A person begins to write letters to the editor, and finds that others in the town write supportive letters. He talks to an old friend, or a neighbor, and finds that he too feels the same way.

The time sequence from stage two or three is important to note. These processes usually take place simultaneously. As the individual is being rejected or labeled a deviant by the larger society, he is being accepted by the primary group. This is what furnishes the bond, the integration into a group. If all the individual experienced was opprobrious labeling and a reaction by avoidance, one would expect his behavior to be extinguished.[10] However, since immediately after the labeling the deviant experiences reinforcement and attention from others, his behavior is "learned," and it continues. (This process is similar to that discussed by Sutherland when he deals with the differential association process and the "learning" of criminal behavior.)[11]

Finally, the individual becomes a member of a group which develops or has already developed an ideology which further supports these deviant acts. In some cases, as Becker has indicated, the more deviant the group, the greater the tendency for it to have an ideology which explains why they are "right" and the dominant society "wrong." As those who have directed barbs at rightist groups have seen, there is a tendency on the part of these people to see all criticism directed their way as being communist-inspired. The person who is vocal and is attacked by the dominant society is esteemed because this proves that he is "hurting the Communists." Therefore, the more deviant the person becomes in terms of the dominant society, the more prestige he may obtain in the smaller society of the rightist organization. The group that the individual joins gives a focus to his frustrations and deviant impulses and rewards him specifically because he had these impulses and acts on them.

John Lofland and Rodney Stark have developed a model to explain the process by which people were converted to a millenarian cult called the Divine Precepts. The seven steps which they saw as necessary for conversion involve a process whereby a person must:

1. experience enduring and recognized tensions,
2. within a religious problem-solving context,
3. so that he sees himself as a seeker,
4. encounters the Divine Precepts at a turning point in his life,
5. forms an effective bond with the members of the group,
6. thereby reducing extra-cult attachments or neutralizing them,
7. and, simultaneously is exposed to intensive interaction within the cult.[12]

If one eliminates the religious referents in this model, then it is possible to see the close parallels between the process Lofland and Stark describe and that which we have outlined. A person first feels some general social need. Something in his life is bothering him, and he wants to solve the problem. He meets someone, or may already have a friend, who is sympathetic to his problem and tells the "convert" that he belongs to a group that can help him. As bonds of friendship are formed in the group, ties are weakened or severed in the larger community. The greater the commitment which must be shown to the group, the greater will be the isolation from the larger society.

The tensions which Lofland and Stark describe as necessary for conversion can be manifold for the person in the Center. As we noted, people are isolated by virtue of age. Men and women who have had their family unit disrupted by death, or even by the simple fact of the children leaving home for college or to get married, have a set of old behavior patterns which no longer fit a new situation. An adaptation must be made. A person who is downwardly mobile, or poor, experiences obvious tensions in a society geared to reward only the successful.

However, it could be argued with some justification that everyone in a society experiences frustrations and tensions, but everyone doesn't become a radical rightist or join the Divine Precepts. That brings up the question of alternatives. All of the models presented so far imply that deviance is the mode of behavior when other "legitimate" outlets are not available. For the middle-class person who never experiences any dramatic changes in his life the methods of dealing with stress or tension are routinized. The middle-class person may have open to him a variety of intermediate associations, whether they be the country club or the local Democratic or Republican clubs in which he can engage in what seems to him meaningful contact with others. Sometimes, however, a person cannot find satisfaction in his immediate environment. What would have been the normally acceptable alternatives are not present. Alternatives may become limited for a person when the death of a spouse limits participation in activities that call for couples. Or the person may move to another city and have to seek out new relationships which demand new forms of behavior. (A case in point would be the rural person who becomes an urban dweller.) Under circumstances such as these, then, the person will accept the alternative that is available to him. The alternatives that he has at his disposal will of course vary with such standard variables as age, sex, socioeconomic status, and race. The *availability* of a particular group, when the individual has the *impulse* to join, determines the group he will join.

9

THE FUTURE OF THE RIGHT?

The movement that we have described has become history. But where have the people gone, and what is the Center doing now? Were the social forces that sustained the radical right in the United States unique to one period of time, or should we expect such a movement to continue to be viable?

In some respects the conditions which gave rise to the radical right in the late fifties and early sixties are still with us. There are economic conditions plaguing those who have retired on fixed incomes, who have been thrown out of work, and, of course, anybody affected by inflation. The international role of the United States seems to be changing in ways most people cannot explain. As we indicated previously, one of the issues for the radical right in the 1960s was our failure to win in Korea. Certainly our failure to win a decisive military victory in Vietnam is a parallel instance. Then, after Watergate, and the attendant loss in the public's confidence in government at all levels, the circumstances could have called for a resurgence of the right. Where has the right gone? Why hasn't it been heard from?

There have been general social trends that have contributed to the right's lack of visibility as well as credibility. One factor was well expressed by a conservative who said, "It's hard to continue to hate." One of the things that sustained the right was the monistic explanation that Communists were behind the problems of the country. Yet the supposed threat of an internal Communist conspiracy has been difficult to demonstrate, and has not been an issue which people have rallied around.

Related to the idea of an internal threat is the possibility of an external one. The traditional nemeses of the right—the Soviet Union and the People's Republic of China—have been recognized by the government, and a conservative one at that. Economic and political interests have dictated the détente with the Soviets and the rapprochement with the People's Republic. Taiwan was forgotten by the public soon after China took her seat in the United Nations.

A paradox here has further weakened the base of support for the right. We have had a conservative Republican administration being hard on the left domestically, thereby absolving itself of criticism from the right; and being "soft" on the international left, simply confusing a larger part of the right. One of the issues of the right during the rise of the student left and the civil rights movement in this country was that these were really groups controlled by Communists because our soft liberal government allowed it to happen. But with the Nixon Administration there was a definite move to the right. The government did persecute leftist groups, did indict numerous people for conspiracy, and did claim that many demonstrations were the product of hard-core activists, much to the satisfaction of rightists in the United States. The effect of this was, then, to absorb a significant portion of the discontent that had existed on the right.

On the other hand, as we have noted, this same government instituted the softening of relations with major communist powers. It also instituted wage-and-price controls, and other economic policies unacceptable to the traditional right. What seemed to operate here, then, was the development of cross-pressures for many rightists; and the effect was political apathy on the right. Second, it must be remembered that a rightist organization cannot support its activities without funds. For large contributors to the Right, the Nixon policies were perfectly acceptable because the developments in foreign policy would ultimately aid business in the United States. Why didn't the little man continue to contribute? As has been suggested, the person at the bottom of the socioeconomic ladder tends to respond to immediate threats and issues—students, minorities, crime in the streets, and a decay of morals. The issues of foreign policy are remote to him, and if the national government deals with his immediate problems, or he thinks it does, the other issues become almost irrelevant for him.

The sources of cross-pressure were more ubiquitous than simply a conflict between the government's domestic policies and their foreign policies from the perspective of the right. First, there was Richard Nixon himself, who was an early anti-communist hero, and who now seemed to play the role as the leader of the move to the Left in foreign policy. Another factor related to Nixon's role in Watergate. One of the sources of moral strength for the Right had been the idea that if the free market and the business ethic should dominate, everything would work out for the good of the country. Yet Watergate seemed to indicate to many that one of their own heroes did not hold in esteem the same principles that they did.

Business as well as business leaders had often been portrayed in rightist literature as being imbued with the highest principles, and business leadership was often implicitly equated with moral leadership. Big business was supposed to be a panacea for the evils of communism; and the free enterprise system, if left alone, was supposed to solve our major problems. Yet the oil crisis which had been partly generated by big business, the grain deal with the Soviet Union, and similar incidents, served to negate these basic ideas. For it was big business in collusion with government officials which worked to subvert the principles of the free enterprise system, and which cost the average man money. Confusion and despair produced cross-pressure which mitigated against involvement in political groups.

Another national factor that affected the Right was the

media. The media can and do sustain support for social movements by simply bringing a group and its ideology before the public and making them think about it. The Freedom Center got its start in Portland, Oregon, primarily because of the coverage given to their activities in the local paper, and then the television coverage of their request to solicit funds door-to-door. With the advent of the civil rights movement, and the student movement in the 1960s, the right was, quite simply, no longer interesting news. The left was for an extended period the only group providing any organized opposition to the war in Vietnam, and the only group providing an explanation for it. This made news. The explanations that the Right may have had were often too bizarre to receive attention —for example, the government got us into Vietnam in order to weaken the country for a Communist takeover—or these explanations weren't any different from those being offered by members of the government such as, we're in Vietnam to protect democracy. These factors, then, seriously undermined the basis of support for the Right on a national level: the lack of traditional enemies, the move of the government toward the right, the development of cross-pressures, and the media's lack of interest in the right.

On the local level, there were additional factors responsible for a decline in the fortunes of the Freedom Center. Any social movement that hopes to be successful must deal with the issue of how to attract new recruits. If they are to encourage the second generation, they must usually change the requirements for membership. In the case of the Freedom Center this would have meant that the group would have had to move in a more middle-class direction. But, of course, if this had happened, the number of other groups available to the potential recruit would have become greater, and the Center would have lost its uniqueness. And there was nothing in the Center's dogma and program that would have made it particularly attractive to a younger generation, or to one more affluent. In the 1960s the Center was fulfilling a basic social, rather than ideological, need of its adherents. A young person's social needs would not have been met in this organization even if his ideological needs were, which is also doubtful, because the Center explained the contemporary world in terms of a fundamentalistic and militant anti-communistic rhetoric. A significant portion of the young population was polarized to the right by the civil rights movement and the student demonstrations, but they responded to the populist, anti-establishment rhetoric of George Wallace. The Freedom Center failed to find a significant number of new recruits, and it failed to generate new issues. The effect was a decline in the organization. On occasion, the group has tried to capture control of the state Republican party, but these efforts, which are essentially the work of Walter Huss and a few other loyalists, most of whom are not Freedom Center members, have failed.

This is a movement, then, that has failed; whose members have died, or have gone on to other issues. But that does not mean that future movements of a similar nature will not arise, for, as we have argued, the forces that contribute to the development of extremist politics are inherent in the body politic. There will always be people positioned on the fringes of society who will welcome simplistic explanations coupled with a conspiracy theory. And, if we can venture to make predictions, the extent to which people are able to explain the troubles of former President Nixon as flowing from a "conspiracy" of the left, the media, and so on, is the extent to which we can expect a resurgence of the Right. The Right does depend on a Left for its existence, as there must be an enemy to which the organizers of rightist movements must be able to point. If the government moves toward the left, or it can be argued that it has, then the Right once again becomes viable.

American institutions are in difficult straits, as people have turned against them or are withholding their judgment. Public opinion polls indicate a deep apathy on the part of the general population, and a distrust toward the government and economic, educational, and religious institutions. People seem to be waiting for someone to tell them who to blame for the current state of affairs. The Right waits.

APPENDIX

TABLE A.1

DISTRIBUTION OF RIGHTISTS BY CENSUS REGION
(In Percent)

REGION	NATIONAL POPULATION	WARTENBURG AND THIELENS STUDY	McEVOY STUDY	McNALL STUDY
California	8.8	33	29	34
Other Far West	6.8	9	11	9
South	30.7	29	29	22
North Central	28.8	18	19	19
Northeast	24.9	11	10	16
Unknown			2	
Totals	100.0	100.0	100.0	100.0

Source: Data shown above for both the Wartenburg and Thielens study and the McEvoy study comes from James McEvoy, p. 17.

TABLE A.2

RELATIONSHIP OF SELECTED ITEMS AND MEMBERSHIP IN JOHN BIRCH SOCIETY ON A STATE BASIS

VARIABLES	1	2	3	4	5	6	7	8	9
1. Percent of total population who are Protestants[a]		.77	.31	−.24	−.23	−.49	−.40	−.35	−.26
2. Percent Protestant according to religious faith[b]			.51	−.21	−.11	−.46	−.50	−.37	−.13
3. Percent of Protestants who are Fundamentalists[c]				−.26	−.29	−.38	−.21	−.26	−.07
4. Migration[d]					.52	−.04	.67	.67	.51
5. Suicide[e]						.11	.34	.50	.27
6. Age[f]							.04	.11	−.07
7. Theft[g]								.82	.38
8. Larceny[h]									.48
9. Membership in Birch Society[i]									

a. Percent of total population who are Protestants is the population of each state in 1950 divided into the total number of Protestants. Source: **Churches and Church Membership in the United States.** Series A, No. 3, Table 4. (New York, National Council of the Churches of Christ in the U.S.A., 1956).

b. Percent Protestant according to religious faith refers to the number of Protestants in a given state divided by all reported church members for that state. Source: **Churches and Church Membership,** Series A, No. 4, Table 7.

c. Percent of Protestants who are Fundamentalists was calculated by adding the number of reported church members for the Fundamentalist churches in a given state and dividing by the total reported Protestant church members. Groups classified as Fundamentalist were such groups as: Seventh-Day Adventists, Assemblies of God, Church of God, Church of the Nazarene, United Brethren, Pentecostal Holiness, and International Church of the Foursquare Gospel. Source: **Churches and Church Membership,** Series B, Nos. 5, 6, 7, and 8, Table 12.

d. Migration refers to the percent of total population change between 1950 and 1960. Source: U.S. Bureau of the Census. **Statistical Abstract of the United States: 1960** (81st ed.), Washington, D.C., 1960.

e. Suicide refers to the number of suicides in a given state per million population. Source: U.S. Bureau of the Census. **Vital Statistics of the United States: 1960,** Washington, D.C., 1960.

f. Age refers to the median age of the population for a given state. Source: U.S. Bureau of the Census. **U.S. Census of Population: 1960, Characteristics of the Population,** Washington, D.C., 1963.

g. Theft refers to the number of known offenses exceeding $50 for a given state per 100,000 population. Source: **Uniform Crime Reports, 1960.**

h. Larceny refers to a number of known offenses exceeding $50 for a given state per 100,000 population. Source: **Statistical Abstracts of the United States: 1962.**

i. Membership in the John Birch Society refers to the McNall analysis of 1600 letters.

TABLE A.3

**COMPARISON OF FIVE COUNTIES IN WHICH BIRCHERS ARE
CONCENTRATED WITHIN THE LARGER STATE OF CALIFORNIA
(In Percent)**

COUNTY	INCREASE IN POPU-LATION 1950-1960	FOREIGN BORN	MEDIAN YEARS OF SCHOOL	RATE OF UN-EMPLOY-MENT	NUMBER OF PROFES-SIONALS	MEDIAN FAMILY INCOME
Los Angeles	45.5	9.5	12.1	5.7	14.8	$7046
San Bernardino	78.8	5.7	11.7	6.2	10.7	5998
San Diego	85.5	6.3	12.1	6.2	15.2	6545
Santa Barbara	72.0	9.9	12.2	3.6	14.9	6823
Santa Clara	121.1	7.9	12.2	4.6	19.2	7417
CALIFORNIA	48.5	8.5	12.1	6.1	13.5	6726

Source: U.S. Bureau of the Census. **U.S. Census of Population: 1960, Vol. 1, Characteristics of the Population.** Part 6, California. U.S. Government Printing Office, Washington, D.C., 1963.

TABLE A.4

SOCIAL STATUS AREAS IN WHICH CENTER MEMBERS RESIDE

(High Status)				Scale Value				(Low Status)	
	0	1	2	3	4	5	6	7	T
Number of members	23	29	25	34	37	37	46	35	266
Percentage of members	8.65	10.90	9.40	12.78	13.91	13.91	17.29	13.16	100
Percentage of total population	11.21	15.53	11.27	11.18	14.62	12.03	13.33	10.83	100
Percentage difference	−2.56	−4.63	−1.87	+1.60	−.71	+1.88	+3.96	+2.33	

$X^2=12.00$ P > .05. Difference between expected and observed number of members.

APPENDIX

TABLE A.5

AREAS OF SOCIAL DISORGANIZATION AND RESIDENCE OF CENTER MEMBERS

(Low Disorganization)						(High Disorganization)		
0	1	2	3	4	5	6	7	T
Number of members								
22	32	35	34	38	41	35	29	266
Percentage of members								
8.27	12.03	13.16	12.78	14.28	15.41	13.16	10.61	100
Percentage of total population								
11.97	14.29	13.58	11.81	14.41	12.06	12.05	9.83	100
Percentage difference								
−3.50	−2.26	−.42	+.97	−.13	+3.35	+1.11	+1.08	

$x^2 = 7.45$ P > .05. Difference between observed and expected number of members.

TABLE A.6

VOTES FOR PRESIDENTIAL CANDIDATES IN 1964
(In Percentages)

	Centerites	Other Rightists
Goldwater	84	92
Johnson	09	04
Did Not Vote	05	02
Refused to Say	—	02
Other Candidate	02	—
T	100%	100%
N	56	53

186

NOTES

CHAPTER 1

1. Seymour Martin Lipset and Earl Raab, *The Politics of Unreason* (New York, Harper and Row, 1970), pp. 10–11.

2. John H. Bunzel, *Anti-Politics in America* (New York, Alfred A. Knopf, Inc., 1967).

3. Lipset and Raab, *op. cit.*, p. 12.

4. *Ibid.*, p. 14.

5. Everett C. Ladd, Jr., "The Radical Right: The White-Collar Extremists," *The South Atlantic Quarterly*, Vol. 65 (Summer 1966), p. 323.

6. Samuel A. Stouffer, *Communism, Conformity and Civil Liberties* (New York, John Wiley & Sons, Inc., 1966).

7. Neil J. Smelser, *The Theory of Collective Behavior* (New York, The Free Press, 1963).

8. Lipset and Raab, p. 260.

9. Joseph R. Gusfield, *Symbolic Crusade: Status Politics and the American Temperance Movement* (Urbana, Illinois, University of Illinois Press, 1963), p. 19.

CHAPTER 2

1. Portland City Council, "Hearings on Application of Free-

NOTES

dom Center to Solicit Funds," Portland, Oregon (May 11, 1961).

2. Communiqué from the Eugene Water and Electric Board to the Portland City Council.

3. Personal discussion with a University of Oregon faculty member (September 1964).

4. Portland City Council Hearings (May 11, 1961).

5. From a report filed with the Portland City Council (approximately February 1961).

6. *Freedom Crusader,* Vol. 1 (January 1, 1960), pp. 1 and 4.

7. Walter Huss, letter in the *Medford Mail Tribune* (July 27, 1964).

8. Hans Gerth and C. Wright Mills, *From Max Weber: Essays in Sociology* (New York, Oxford University Press, 1958).

9. Gerald D. Berreman, "Caste in India and the United States," *American Journal of Sociology,* Vol. 66 (September 1960), pp. 120–27.

10. Leon Festinger, Henry Riecken, and Stanley Schacter, *When Prophecy Fails* (Minneapolis, University of Minnesota Press, 1956).

11. From a mimeographed letter dated February 16, 1961.

12. Portland City Council Hearings (May 11, 1961). Author's italics.

13. Arnold Forster and Benjamin R. Epstein, *Danger on the Right* (New York, Random House, 1964), p. 76.

14. Michael P. Fogarty, *Christian Democracy in Western Europe* (London, Routledge and Kegan Paul, 1957).

15. Leo Pfeffer, *Creeds in Competition* (New York, Harper and Row, 1958).

16. Will Herberg, *Protestant, Catholic, Jew* (New York, Doubleday Anchor, 1960).

17. J. Allen Broyles, *The John Birch Society: Anatomy of a Protest* (Boston, Beacon Press, 1964), pp. 46–47.

18. *Center Fax* (June 1961), p. 10.

19. Broyles, *op. cit.,* p. 47.

188

CHAPTER 3

1. This ideal schema is made up of divisions which the Husses actually tried to develop or maintain. It was pieced together from conversations with them and from their publications that dealt with the organization's structure.

2. Rosalie Huss, undated letter (approximately April 1965).

3. "Freedom or Communism, Which Will It Be?" undated pamphlet. Freedom Center, late 1961.

4. *Freedom Crusader* (January 1, 1960), pp. 1 and 4.

5. "Corporation Papers," Freedom Crusade International (Portland, Oregon, January 3, 1961).

6. Freedom Crusade International, mimeographed leaflet (January 17, 1961).

7. *Oregonian* (October 6, 1961).

8. *Center Fax,* 1 (November and December 1961), p. 5.

9. *Ibid.*

10. *Ibid.*

11. *Freedom Crusader,* 1 (January 1, 1960), p. 4.

12. *Ibid.*

13. *Freedom Crusader,* 1 (December 1960), p. 6.

14. Adapted from an advertisement distributed by the Center in 1960.

15. If I correctly understood the complicated events in 1965, Freedom Center International, Inc., formerly called Freedom Crusade International, Inc., which was the adult education branch of Oregon Christian Schools, Inc., a non-profit organization, was part of a "defunct" organization. Huss claimed that the tax exemption of the Center came from the Center's being part of this school, but there was no school. The post office also cut off the Center's non-profit organization rates. Finally, a letter from the Oregon State Tax Commission, dated March 2, 1961, stated that: "I find that Freedom Crusade, P.O. Box 4344, Portland, Oregon, has never made application to the State Tax Commission for exemption from the corporation excise tax as a charitable, educational, scientific or literary organization."

16. *Freedom Crusader,* 1 (December 1960), p. 6.

17. *Ibid.,* p. 7.

18. Taken from an invitation (December 1960).

19. Portland City Council Hearings (May 11, 1961).

20. Portland City Council Hearings (December 22, 1960).

21. *Ibid.*

22. Portland City Council Hearings (January 26, 1961).

23. Letter dated February 16, 1961.

24. Portland City Council Hearings (February 16, 1961). Adapted from the proceedings.

25. *Ibid.*

26. *Ibid.*

27. *Oregonian* (February 9, 1961).

28. Portland Bureau of Police, Officer's Report, #5503 (February 4, 1961).

29. Walter Huss, letter dated February 16, 1961.

30. Letter dated April 20, 1961.

31. "Baker's Dozen," *Oregon Journal* (April 4, 1962).

32. *Oregonian* (April 7, 1961).

33. *Oregon Journal* (May 8, 1961).

34. Portland City Council Hearings (May 11, 1961).

35. Edmund Crump, National Party of America (Portland, Oregon, February 9, 1965).

36. *Center Fax,* Vol. 1, No. 5 (August 1961), p. 12.

37. From an undated pamphlet (1962).

38. *American Eagle,* 1 (January 1962), p. 5.

39. All quotations are taken from letters written to President Flemming during February 1962.

40. "Freedom Center," Section 1, Oregon, Group Research, Inc. (Washington, D.C., 1964), p. 2.

41. Adapted from an ad in the *National Eagle,* 1 (June 1962), p. 6.

42. Walter Huss, letter dated September 1962.

43. *National Eagle,* 1 (July 1962), p. 5.

44. Congressman James B. Utt, "Washington Report" (Washington, D.C., n.d.).

45. C. W. Burpo, *An Angry American* (Glendale, California, The Church Press).

46. *National Eagle,* 2 (May 1963), p. 2.

47. *Oregon Journal* (November 3, 1963).

48. *Oregonian* (May 1, 1964).

49. Taken from a campaign brochure.

50. *National Eagle,* 3 (June 1964), p. 1.

51. *Ibid.*

52. *National Eagle,* 3 (July 4, 1964), pp. 1–4.

53. *Ibid.,* p. 4.

54. Eric Allen, Jr., "Whoop It Up," editorial in *Medford Mail Tribune* (July 10, 1964).

55. Walter Huss, letter dated Christmas 1964.

CHAPTER 4

1. Rudolph Heberle, *Social Movements* (New York, Appleton-Century-Crofts, 1951), p. 6.

2. Jerome Davis, *Contemporary Social Movements* (New York, Appleton-Century-Crofts, 1930), pp. 18–19.

3. *Freedom Crusader,* 1 (Januray 1, 1960), pp. 1 and 4.

4. *Ibid.,* p. 4.

5. *Freedom Crusader,* 1 (December 1960), p. 6.

6. J. Allen Broyles, *The John Birch Society: Anatomy of a Protest* (Boston, Beacon Press, 1962).

7. Robert Welch, *The Blue Book of the John Birch Society* (Belmont, The John Birch Society, 1959), pp. 75–76.

8. *Ibid.,* p. 76.

9. Broyles, p. 82.

10. H. Richard Niebuhr, *The Social Sources of Denominationalism* (New York, Meridian Books, Inc., 1957).

11. *Ibid.,* pp. 19–20.

12. Bryan R. Wilson, "An Analysis of Sect Development," *American Sociological Review,* 24 (February 1959), pp. 3–15.

13. *American Eagle,* 1 (January 1962), p. 3.

14. *Ibid.,* p. 8.

15. *Ibid.,* p. 6.

16. *Ibid.,* p. 2.

17. *American Eagle,* 1 (February 1962), p. 1.

18. *American Eagle,* 1 (March 1962), p. 1.

19. *National Eagle,* 1 (September 1962), p. 1.

20. Arnold L. Green, "The Ideology of Anti-Fluoridation Leaders," *The Journal of Social Issues,* 17 (1961), p. 24.

21. In the interview Center members were asked how they would vote on the fluoridation issue. Eighty-six percent of the Center members were opposed to fluoridation of the water supply with 10 percent willing to vote for it, and 4 percent not sure.

22. *American Eagle,* 1 (February 1962), p. 7.

23. *National Eagle,* 2 (February–March 1963), p. 5.

24. *National Eagle,* 1 (August 1962), p. 2.

25. A question put to Center members was: "Do you believe that as philosophies of government modern liberalism, socialism and communism are all essentially the same?" Seventy-five percent of Center members said, "Yes."

26. *Center Fax,* 1 (June 1961), p. 3.

27. *National Eagle,* 1 (August 1962), p. 6.

28. *American Eagle,* 1 (September 1962), p. 2.

29. *Center Fax,* 1 (June 1961), p. 3.

30. *Freedom Crusader,* 1 (January 1,1960), p. 1.

31. Walter Huss, letter dated June 11, 1962.

32. Articles of Incorporation.

33. *Freedom Crusader,* 1 (January 1, 1960), p. 3.

34. Walter Huss, mimeographed letter dated February 27, 1961.

35. According to a report made by the National Council of the Churches of Christ, Oregon had the lowest percentage of reported church membership of any state. Using the 1950 census data, the reported church membership as a percen-

tage of the total population for the Pacific Coast states for all major faiths was: California, 40.7 percent; Oregon, 27.7 percent; and Washington, 30.5 percent. An examination of reports based on the 1960 and 1970 census data indicates that this situation still prevails. These figures come from: *Churches and Church Membership in the United States,* Series A, No. 3 (New York, National Council of Churches of Christ in the U.S.A., 1956).

36. *The John Birch Society:* A Report (Belmont, The John Birch Society), p. 5.

37. *Ibid.,* p. 16.

38. Robert Welch, *Blue Book,* pp. 140–50.

39. Broyles, p. 122.

40. Will Herberg, *Protestant, Catholic, Jew* (New York, Doubleday & Company, Inc., 1960).

41. Peter L. Berger, *The Noise of Solemn Assemblies* (New York, Doubleday & Company, Inc., 1961).

42. *Ibid.,* p. 41.

43. Hans Gerth and C. Wright Mills, *From Max Weber: Essays in Sociology* (New York, Oxford University Press, 1958).

44. Ernst Troeltsch, *The Social Teaching of the Christian Churches,* Vol. 1, trans. by Olive Wyon with an introduction by Richard Niebuhr (New York, Harper Torchbooks, 1960).

45. Russell R. Dynes, "Church-Sect Typology and Socio-Economic Status," *American Sociological Review,* 20 (October 1955), pp. 555–60.

46. Elmer T. Clark, *The Small Sects in America* (New York, Abingdon-Cokesbury Press, 1949), pp. 22–24.

47. J. Milton Yinger, *Religion, Society and the Individual* (New York, The Macmillan Company, 1957), pp. 144–55.

48. *Ibid.,* p. 155.

49. Gerth and Mills, *op. cit.,* pp. 151–52.

50. Yinger, *op. cit.,* pp. 144–55.

51. J. S. Burgess, "The Study of Modern Social Movements as a Means for Clarifying the Process of Social Action," *Social Forces,* 22 (1944), p. 269.

52. Theodore Able, "The Pattern of a Successful Political Movement," *American Sociological Review,* 2 (June 1937), p. 347.

53. Yinger, *op. cit.,* p. 152.

CHAPTER 5

1. From a meeting in Eugene, Oregon, July 1962.

2. *National Eagle,* 2 (April 1963), p. 4.

3. *American Eagle,* 1 (January 1962), p. 5.

4. Walter Huss, mimeographed letter, Christmas 1964. Author's italics.

CHAPTER 6

1. See for instance: Theodore R. Anderson and Janice A. Egeland, "Spatial Aspects of Social Area Analysis," *American Sociological Review,* 26 (June 1961), pp. 392–98; Wendell Bell, "The Social Areas of the San Francisco Bay Region," *American Sociological Review,* 18 (February 1953), pp. 39–47; Eshref Shevky and Marilyn Williams, *The Social Areas of Los Angeles, Analysis and Typology* (Berkeley, California, University of California Press, 1949).

2. Clifford R. Shaw and Henry D. McKay, *Juvenile Delinquency in Urban Areas* (Chicago, University of Chicago Press, 1942).

3. The problems of dealing with ecological correlations have been discussed by William S. Robinson, "Ecological Correlations and the Behavior of Individuals," *American Sociological Review,* 15 (June 1950), pp. 351–57.

4. Bulletin for November (Belmont, Massachusetts, The John Birch Society, November 5, 1964).

5. *Ibid.*

6. Hannah Wartenburg and Wagner Thielens, Jr., *Against the United Nations: A Letter Writing Campaign by the Birch Movement* (New York, Columbia University Bureau of Applied Social Research, 1964, mimeographed).

7. James McEvoy, *Letters from the Right: Content-Analysis of a Letter Writing Campaign* (Ann Arbor, Michigan, University of Michigan Center for Research on Utilization of Scientific Knowledge, 1966, mimeographed).

8. It should be noted that the index of disorganization is being taken as an operational indicator of mass society. For our

purposes, disruption of stable events which allows a person to locate reference points to validate himself and meet his social needs, is seen as that which creates a mass society. There are a variety of other phenomena which have been seen as the *result* of mass society—for example, alienation, anomie, and so forth. It is, however, difficult to measure these phenomena on a societal level, and claim that a mass society does, or does not exist.

9. Émile Durkheim, *Suicide,* trans. by John A. Spaulding and George Simpson (New York, The Free Press, 1951).

10. Kai T. Erickson, "Notes on the Sociology of Deviance," *Social Problems,* 9 (1962), pp. 307–14.

11. Seymour Martin Lipset, "Three Decades of the Radical Right: Coughlinites, McCarthyites, and Birchers," in Daniel Bell, ed., *The Radical Right* (New York, Doubleday & Company, Inc., 1963).

12. That 32 percent of the Birchers in California live outside of the areas characterized by extremely high rates of population growth still does not mean that disorganization does not play its part in explaining where the remainder are located. It must be remembered that California itself experienced a more rapid rate of growth between 1950 and 1960 than did the other states in the country.

13. The percentage of the labor force unemployed was computed by dividing all of those males listed as unemployed by the total civilian labor force for any given census tract. These same variables have been used by a variety of researchers in constructing indices of social status based on census tract data. See for example: Calvin F. Schmid, "Generalizations Concerning the Ecology of the American City," *American Sociological Review,* 15 (April 1950), pp. 264–81; and Eshref Shevky and Wendell Bell, *Social Area Analysis, Theory, Illustrative Application and Computational Procedures* (Stanford, California, Stanford University Press, 1955).

14. The percentage of dwelling units deteriorating and dilapidated was computed by dividing the total number of dwelling units in these conditions by the total number of dwelling units for the census tract. The rate of family disruption was computed by adding together the sums of those divorced, widowed, and separated and dividing it by the total population age fourteen and over. It was decided to compute this latter figure only for the white population, even when the non-white population in the census tract was larger than the

white. This was because the rates for family disruption were similar for both whites and non-whites in the same census tract.

15. David F. Aberle, *The Peyote Religion Among the Navaho,* Publication #42 (New York, Wenner-Gren Foundation for Anthropological Research, Inc., 1966), p. 31.

16. For a discussion of the theory of intervening opportunities, see: Samuel A. Stouffer, "Intervening Opportunities: A Theory Relating Mobility and Distance," *American Sociological Review,* 5 (December 1940), pp. 845–67.

CHAPTER 7

1. Unless otherwise indicated, the percentages reported for Centerites and other rightists refer to a base N of fifty-six Centerites and fifty-three other rightists.

2. Murry C. Havens, "The Radical Right in the Southwest: Community Response to Shifting Socio-Economic Patterns" (University of Texas, September 1964), p. 14.

3. This particular combination of variables has found great support among Hollingshead and his students. For a discussion of the occupational scale see A. B. Hollingshead, *Index of Social Position.* Unpublished manuscript, Department of Sociology, Yale University. For a discussion of the combination of Hollingshead's occupational scale and an "educational" scale, see Robert A. Ellis, W. Clayton Lane, and Virginia Olesen, "The Index of Class Position: An Improved Measure of Stratification," *American Sociological Review,* 28 (April 1, 1963), pp. 271–77.

In deriving the social class for our respondents we followed the rule of taking husband's occupation, whether or not the wife who may have been interviewed was working herself. This was then combined with the respondent's education.

4. See especially Michael Harrington, *The Other America* (Baltimore, Penguin Books, 1964); Genevieve Knupfer, "Portrait of the Underdog," *The Public Opinion Quarterly,* II (Spring 1947), pp. 103–14; and Joan Moore, "Exclusiveness and Ethnocentrism in a Metropolitan Upper-Class Agency," *Pacific Sociological Review,* 5 (Spring 1962), pp. 16–20.

5. See Milton M. Gordon, *Social Class in American Sociology* (New York, McGraw-Hill, 1963), for a discussion of self-rating techniques.

6. Paul F. Lazarsfeld, Bernard Berelson, and Hazel Gaudet, *The People's Choice* (New York, Columbia University Press, 1948).

7. S. M. Lipset and others, "The Psychology of Voting: An Analysis of Political Behavior," in G. Lindzey, ed., *Handbook of Social Psychology* (Reading, Addison-Wesley, 1954).

8. S. M. Lipset, *Political Man* (New York, Doubleday Anchor, (1963), p. 92.

9. *Ibid.,* p. 97.

10. Gerhard Lenski, *The Religious Factor* (New York, Doubleday Anchor, 1963), p. 223.

11. Lipset, *op. cit.,* p. 116.

12. T. W. Adorno and others, *The Authoritarian Personality* (New York, Harper and Brothers, 1950).

13. Howard Becker, "The Regimented Man: Interviews with German Officials Under the Nazis," *Social Forces* (October 1949), pp. 19–24.

14. This comparison is for analytic purposes only and does not imply that Centerites are Nazis.

CHAPTER 8

1. Howard S. Becker, *Outsiders* (Glencoe, The Free Press, 1963).

2. *Ibid.,* pp. 1–25.

3. The following information also comes from Becker's book.

4. *Ibid.,* p. 25.

5. *Ibid.,* p. 27.

6. See note 3 of chapter 7.

7. U.S. Bureau of the Census, *Statistical Abstract of the United States* (Washington, D.C., 1960), 81st ed.

8. See p. 143 describing Hollingshead's measure.

9. From a Center publication, October 1962.

10. I am indebted to Daniel Glaser for this observation.

11. Edwin H. Sutherland and Donald R. Cressey, *Principles of Criminology* (Philadelphia, Lippincott, 1966), chapter 13.

NOTES

12. Adapted from John Lofland and Rodney Stark, "Becoming a World Saver: A Theory of Conversion to a Deviant Perspective," *American Sociological Review,* 30 (December 1965), pp. 862–75.

INDEX

Aberle, David F., 135
Able, Theodore, 105
Adam, Patrick D., 38
Adorno, Theodore W., 160
Allen, Eric, 23, 66, 69
Allen, Robert, 41
American Protective Association, 10
American way of life, 13–14, 29, 37, 57, 96
Anderson, Theodore R., 121
Anti-Catholicism, 14
Anti-Masons, 9
Anti-politics, 10
Anti-semitism, 14, 52, 53–54, 62
Arens, Richard, 41
Authoritarianism, 156–163
Availability, 132, 135, 138, 177

Backlash, 14
Bauer, Werner, 38
Becker, Howard, 161–163, 167–168, 175
Bell, Daniel, 131
Bell, Wendel, 121, 133
Berger, Peter, 100
Berreman, Gerald D., 23–24
Bisel, James, 33–34, 116, 117
Bonhomme, George, 38–39
Boy Scouts of America, 174
Boyle, Donzella Cross, 41
Brown, Faith, 39
Brown, Wilmer, 40

Broyles, J. Allen, 29, 31, 79, 82
Bryan, William Jennings, 100
Bunzel, John H., 10
Burgess, J. S., 105
Burpo, Charles W., 28, 61, 62, 112

Caradja, "Princess" Catherine, 40
Career of radical rightist, 167–177
Cascade College, 40
Castro, Fidel, 90
Chamberlain, Bob, 37
Chamberlain, William, 51
Chandler, (Mrs.) Norman, 122
Chiang Kai-shek, 93
Christian Anti-Communist Crusade, 28, 36, 114
Christian Science, 103
Church, 82–86, 99
Cinema Educational Guild, 62, 155
Civil liberties, 13
Civil rights movement, 9, 92, 181
Clark, Elmer T., 101
Committee for Improved Education, 66, 69
Committee for the Protection of the Foreign Born, 51
Conspiracy theory, 10–15, 93, 96, 154, 179
Cook, Florence Reed, 69
Coughlin, Charles E., 10, 12
Continuity in organizations, 26–32

199

Control of members, 26
Cotton, Richard, 24, 155, 160
Cressey, Donald R., 175
Crump, Edmund, 53-54

Davis, Jerome, 75-78
Détente, 179
Deviance, 128, 138, 171
    deviant careers, 167-168, 174-177
Disney, Walt, 122-123
Disorganization, 125-128, 134-138, 171
    areas of, 130-131
    indicators of, 125
    related to rightism, 127
Divine Precepts, 176-177
Doctrinal Populism, 10-11
Dodds, William, 40
Domreis, William, 37
Durkheim, Émile, 101, 126-127, 154
Dynes, Russell R., 101

Earl, James, 44-47, 48, 49
Egeland, Janice A., 121
Eisenhower, Dwight, 80, 159, 174
Ellis, Robert A., 196
Epstein, Benjamin R., 28
Erickson, Kai T., 128, 138
Expressive politics, 15

Facilitating conditions, 172-177
Fagan, Myron C., 62, 155
Fakkema, Mark, 59, 114
Festinger, Leon, 24
Fleming, Arthur, 56, 65
Flett, Austin T., 27
Fluoridation controversy, 90-91
Fogarty, Michael P., 28
Forster, Arnold, 28
Freedom Center
    appeal to youth, 53
    changing themes, 88-94
    characteristic meetings, 16-17
    decline of interest, 59-60, 70-72,
        178-182
    directors, 37
    Freedom Shares, 34, 71
    founding of, 21, 36-39
    historical context, 8-9
    historical development, 39-66
    Lebanon chapter, 40
    letter-writing campaigns, 56
    Medford chapter, 34, 47, 107
    organizational structure, 8-15,
        33-39, 50-51, 78

    radio broadcasts, 40, 42, 45-46, 55,
        61, 77, 88
    reaction of Portland churches to,
        51-52
    relations with Nazi party, 53-54
    revocation of tax-exempt status, 58
    Salem chapter, 39, 76
    source of funds, 30, 108-117
    Troutdale chapter, 42
    use of religious rhetoric, 94-99
Freedom Center members, 139-163
    age of, 169, 173
    areas of residence, 133-145, 173
    attitudes toward world, 141-143
    community backgrounds, 140-141
    family structure, 146-147, 170, 173
    ideology, 154-163, 173
    loyalties to Center, 27-32
    number of, 29-30, 53, 57, 60
    political behavior, 150-154
    religious affiliation, 147-150
    social class, 12, 143-145, 169, 173
Freedom Center publications
    American Eagle, 36, 55, 57, 59, 72,
        89-94, 109, 115, 116
    Center Fax, 37, 39, 54
    Freedom Crusader, 40, 45
    National Eagle, 18, 21, 30, 58
Friendship matrices, 88, 136, 172-173
Fundamentalism and rightism, 10,
    56-57, 129-130, 136, 147-150

Gerber, Roger K., 53-54
Gerth, Hans, 23
Ginsberg, Allen, 18-19
Glaser, Daniel, 175
Goff, Kenneth, 63
Goldwater, Barry, 9, 112, 152, 159
    Goldwater - Miller campaign, 9, 27,
        69, 70, 73, 74, 84, 113, 116,
        147, 150
Gordon, Milton M., 144
Graham, Billy, 159
Green, Arnold L., 90
Green, Edith, 63, 89
Gusfield, Joseph R., 15

Hall, Gus, 55-56, 57-58, 90
Hargis, Billy James, 5, 24, 27-32, 38, 60,
    97-98, 108, 114, 129, 155, 160
Harrington, Michael, 144
Hartle, Barbara, 42
Havens, Murray C., 140
Heberle, Rudolph, 74

Help Fight Communism, Inc., 27
Herberg, Will, 29, 100
Hollingshead, August B., 143
Hoover, Herbert, 159
Hoover, J. Edgar, 112, 160
Horne, Lena, 63
House Committee on Un-American
    Activities, 6, 41, 52, 93
Hunt, H. L., 28
Huss, Rosalie, 19, 31, 33-35, 41, 63,
    72, 83, 88, 108
Huss, Walter, 6-7
    as charismatic leader, 22-26
    debate with Earl, 46
    in organizational structure, 33-35
    personal history, 18-21
    political campaigns, 25, 63-65,
    74, 116, 182

Ideology, 10-15, 154-163, 173
    variations in, 73, 81
    see also American way of life,
    Anti-politics, Blacklash, Civil
    liberties, Conspiracy theory,
    Doctrinal populism, Funda-
    mentalism

John Birch Society, 5, 10, 14, 22, 28,
    29, 31, 52, 79-82, 91, 97-99,
    106-107, 111, 114, 121-131,
    136-138
Johnson, Lyndon, 13, 151-152
Joining rightist organizations
    see Availability, Facilitating con-
    ditions, Friendship matrices,
    Predisposing conditions
Jones, Ernest, 37-38, 55, 61

King, Martin Luther, 54, 89, 92
Klutz, Charles, 39
Know-Nothings, 9
Knupfer, Genevieve, 144
Kornhauser, William, 125
Krater, Jess, 37
Ku Klux Klan, 10, 12, 137

Ladd, Everett C., 12-13
Lazarsfeld, Paul F., 151
Lenski, Gerhard, 157
Lewis and Clark College, 56
Lewis, Fulton, 80
Liberalism, 92
Liberty Amendment, 163
Lindzey, Gardiner, 152

Lipset, Seymour Martin, 10, 131, 152,
    156
Lofland, John, 176-177
Long, Huey, 100
Lush, Lyall, 41, 42

Manion, Clarence, 80, 163
MacArthur, Douglas, 159
McBirnie, Edward, 160
McCarthy, Joseph, 10, 12, 79
McEvoy, James, 124
McIntire, Carl, 5, 24, 28, 30, 61, 108,
    112, 114, 129, 155, 159
McKay, Hamish Scott, 51
McKay, Henry D., 121
McNall, Scott G., 124
McPherson, Aimee Semple, 19
Mackie, William, 51
Mass media, 180-181
Medford Mail Tribune, 23, 66-67
Methodist Federation for Social Action,
    51
Methodological issues, 5-8, 132
Mills, C. Wright, 23
Moore, Joan, 144
Multnomah College, 50
Multnomah School of the Bible, 41, 43

National Association for the Advance-
    ment of Colored People
    (NAACP), 63
National Party of America, 53-54
Navaho, 135
Nazi, 53-54, 161-163
Niebuhr, H. Richard, 83, 85, 88
Nisbet, Robert, 125
Nixon, Richard, 13, 179-180, 182
Noble, John, 40
Northwest Review, 23, 55, 64, 65-69, 90

Operation Water Moccasin, 62
Oregon College of Education, 56, 58
Oregon, University of, 6, 18-19, 56,
    64-69, 117
Oxford Group Movement, 103

Parent Teachers Association, 81
Peronism, 159
Peyotism, 135
Pfeffer, Leo, 29
Philbrick, Herbert, 24, 41, 87, 112, 114
Portland City Council, 22, 25, 37, 44-53
Portland Council of Churches, 52
Portland State University, 55-56

Predisposing conditions, 125, 169–173
Prussion, Karl, 114

Rabb, Earl, 10
Racism, 15, 53–54, 63
Rafferty, Max, 63
Reagan, Ronald, 160
Reed College, 55
Riddell, Robert A., 122
Roberts, Oral, 160
Robinson, Eric L., 52
Robinson, William S., 121
Romulo, Carlos, 97
Rosten, Leo, 149
Rumors, 62

Schiffner, Alexander, 155
Schmale, Olive, 37
Schmid, Calvin F., 133
Schrunk, Terry, 53
Schwarz, Fred, 28, 36, 41, 42, 60, 87, 112, 114
Scott, Aaron M., 48
Sect, 82–86, 99
    sect movement, 104–105
    stages in, 83
    types of, 85–86, 100–107
Shaw, Clifford R., 121
Shevky, Eshref, 121, 133
Simons, Janis, 42
Skousen, Leroy B., 33, 45, 114
Skousen, W. Cleon, 33, 41
Smelser, Neil J., 14
Smith, Gerald L. K., 155, 159
Smoot, Dan, 27, 155
Social movements, 75
    diversification of means, 81
    failures of, 78–79
    stages in, 75–79

Social Status, 133–136, 143–145
    indicators of, 133–134
Stark, Rodney, 176–177
Stebbins, Ellis, 58
Stouffer, Samuel A., 13, 135
Sutherland, Edwin H., 175
Swenson, Ted, 37

Taft, Robert, 160
Thielens, Wagner, 124
Thurmond, Strom, 160
Troeltsch, Ernst, 100–101, 103
Twentieth Century Reformation Hour, 27, 28
United Nations, 14, 62, 81, 91, 102, 122–124, 174
    UNICEF, 60–61, 63
Utt, James B., 44

Vietnam, 178, 181
Voronett, Paul, 45

Wade, Arthur, 37
Walker, Edwin, 159
Wallace, George, 9, 159, 182
Warren, Earl, 14, 47, 81, 174
Wartenburg, Hannah, 124
Watergate, 178, 180
Watts, J. Orville, 41
Weber, Max, 23–25, 100–101, 103
Wedemeyer, Albert C., 43
Welch, Robert, 24, 28, 31, 32, 79–82, 98–99, 122
Whetzel, Frank A., 38
Whitcomb, George, 40
White, Walter, 63
White Citizens Councils, 137
Williams, Marilyn, 121
Wilson, Bryan, R., 85–86

Yinger, Milton J., 103–104